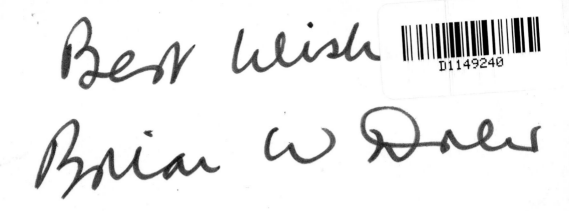

Best Wish[es]

Brian W Drew

A Long Way from Clent

David, Betty Craig & Iain,

May I, through these pages,
share with you, the Joy of the Hills,
and a Special Journey!!!

SPEYSIDE HEATHER.

20.9.2001.

A Long Way from Clent

Brian W. Drew

BREWIN BOOKS

First published in 2001 by
Brewin Books Limited, Doric House, Church Street,
Studley, Warwickshire B80 7LG

British Library Cataloguing – in – Publication Data
A Catalogue record for this book is available from
The British Library

ISBN: 1 85858 194 X

Made and printed by
Warwick Printing Company Limited,
Theatre Street, Warwick, Warwickshire CV34 4DR.

CONTENTS

CHAPTER		Page
1	Pinnacle	1
2	George	7
3	Thomas and Marie-Louise	13
4	Brenda	25
5	Berne	29
6	Hazel	33
7	Contact	37
8	Delay	45
9	Margaret	51
10	Clent	57
11	Strangers Meet	61
12	Angel of Berne	65
13	The Hearse	73
14	Inspiration	79
15	The Chair	89
16	Obsession	97
17	Normality	101
18	Small Talk	105
19	Scotland	109
20	Flying Visit	113

CONTENTS
(continued)

CHAPTER   *Page*

21   Tent Life   121
22   Ten Years to Chamonix   127
23   Aguille   135
24   Blue Peter   141
25   Each Day a Bonus   147
26   Alice and Jack   151
27   Revelation   157
28   The Letter   159
29   Alpina   163
30   Anniversary   169
31   Her Majesty's Pleasure   177
32   Zermatt   181
33   Alan, John and Christopher   187
34   Glen of Weeping   193
35   The Journey Continues   197

The following pictures appear between pages 50 and 51.

i) *Len, Chief Draughtsman at Kaye Alloy Castings Ltd., West Bromwich.*

ii) *Len's great grandad, John Drew. He was pit manager at the Jubilee Pit on the West Bromwich/Handsworth border. The photograph is one of the earliest to be taken down a mine – about 1900. It has been used extensively by the Black Country Museum, which has exhibited it at the entrance to the pit in the museum.*

iii) *Len's grandad, John Drew (Junior) who was working at the coalface by the light of a tallow candle. An early picture of a pit man – taken around 1900 at Jubilee Colliery, West Bromwich.*

iv) *Len, in earlier days when his fitness runs often exceeded 50 miles a week.*

v) *Len and Brenda – pictured in front of the Matterhorn in 1995.*

vi) *Len in his wheelchair in front of the Matterhorn in 1995.*

vii) *A shot of helicopter HB XDA as it was taking off in 1993 – the 21st anniversary of his fall. Len says he had to pay the pilot extra money to get him to stop the blades whilst they were in the formation of "Y" for York!*

viii) *Len in Highland regalia – prompted by his friends Kathy and Ewan Robertson, on a visit to Broadford, Isle of Skye, on 3rd June 1993.*

ix) *20th July 1992. Len studies the climb from the same helicopter that plucked him from the face twenty years earlier. Viewing the shot through a magnifying glass will pick out the Solvay Hut (about half way between the snow shoulder and the bottom of the picture). Len says he may never have attempted the climb if he had seen it from the helicopter beforehand.*

x) *A collage of friends at The English Church, Zermatt.*

xi) *Brenda climbs on fixed ropes above the Hornli Hut – July 1992. Her smile belies the effort she had to put in to reach this spot.*

xii) *A composite picture taken of Len and Alan Plant on the Matterhorn in 1971.*

xiii) *July 1971. Len and Bob Duncan with an unknown Swiss guide, on the precipitous ledge outside the Solvay Hut at a height of 13,200 feet.*

The following pictures appear between pages 146 and 147.

xiv) *Wednesday 28th July 1971 – approaching the Hornli Hutte on the Matterhorn.*

xv) *Len and Alan Plant, on the summit of the Matterhorn. 28th July 1971.*

xvi) *A wooden cross set in stones on the ascent. A moment for contemplation.*

xvii) *Len standing before the North face of the Eiger, July 1972.*

xviii) *Back to the Matterhorn, 23rd July 1972. Roger Massey and part of the team. They agreed to reduce the size of the team to small parties of two and three, to reach the summit.*

xix) *Len's first return to the Alps – 1984.*

xx) *14th July 1990. Len and Brenda, with Lord Hunt, the man who led the first successful expedition to Everest in 1953. This photograph was taken in Zermatt in 1990, on the 125th anniversary of Edward Whymper's first ascent of the Matterhorn.*

xxi) *Evening "Cuillins" on the Isle of Skye. One of Len and Brenda's favourite views. The photograph was taken by Robin Wydell in 1999.*

xxii) *Len's momentous achievement in getting to the top of Kleine Matterhorn is shared with a passing admirer.*

xxiii) *Len with Thomas Aufdenblatten, the man who stayed with him on the mountain through the night of 23rd/24th July 1972.*

xxiv) *Brenda admiring the condition of the helicopter (HB-XDA) that lifted Len from the mountain in 1972. The picture was taken in 1993.*

xxv) *Norman Croucher surprised Len and Brenda in 1993 when he recognised Len's voice in a crowded shopping street in Zermatt. Two climbers with not a useful leg between them.*

xxvi) *Len in chorister's dress at Birmingham Cathedral June 1996. St Hilda's choir sang Evensong. Len has been a member of the choir since he was eight years old.*

xxvii) *On the ascent of the Monte Rosa.*

xxviii) *Thomas and Len, with 'Lucky' Imboden, the first mountain guide to reach Len after his fall.*

xxix) *Resting at 14000 feet 1430 hours.*

xxx) *'Lucky' Imboden, Len and Lucky's brother, Victor. The Imboden brothers found Len, on the Matterhorn in 1972. The occasion was the Centenary of the Mountain Guides Association in 1994.*

xxxi) *A view of the Worcestershire Countryside taken from the four stones on the top of Clent Hills.*

xxxii) *Len with Sir Jimmy Saville MBE at the Robert Jones and Agnes Hunt Spinal Unit, Oswestry. The occasion was the laying of the inaugural stone for the new spinal unit in 1999. PHOTOGRAPH BY DR CLIVE INMAN*

ACKNOWLEDGEMENTS

The author would like to acknowledge the considerable help in compiling this book, he has received from Len and Brenda York. Their efforts in preserving such an exhaustive amount of photographic record and written accounts of their magnificent achievements, has formed the basis for this work.

I am also grateful to the following for contributing some telling chapters:

       Thomas and Elizabeth Aufdenblatten

       Don Haskins

       Maggie

       Marie-Louise

       Jack Yates and his late wife Alice

The Coachhouse Writers of Oldswinford, Stourbridge who have been a continual source of inspiration and enthusiasm for the project.

Sir Chris Bonington CBE for his kindness in providing a foreword, a photograph and priceless encouragement.

Note on Author

B rian Drew grew up in Warley, in a similar environment to that of
Len York, the man who inspired him to write this biography.
Retiring early from a life in the commercial insurance world in 1994,
Brian started writing whilst attending creative writing classes with
Birmingham University School of Continuing Studies (a pleasure
which is ongoing). He has had poems and short stories published by
Coachhouse Writers and *The Black Country Society*.

This, his first major work, follows the miraculous progress of a
man who suffered injuries that would have rendered most people
helpless. It is a story of the infinite courage, superb support and
powerful faith that has resulted in the Len York phenomenon. Len
is a man who has put aside the restrictions of paraplegia, to become
an inspirational figure. A man who uses his own lack of mobility to
create hope for thousands, many of whom are better placed than he.
Len's story will lift you with smiles, charge you with tears and inspire
you with faith.

7th March 2001

For Brenda   To whom Len will never be able adequately
              to convey his lifelong gratitude

For Jan   For her selfless hard work, encouragement and
              for giving the author the privilege of sharing
              the laughter and the tears

FOREWORD
(by Sir Christian Bonington CBE)

I first met Len York in 1967, when I did a talk on "The Eiger – North Face", at Tube Investments Ballroom in Broadwell Road, Oldbury, which was then in Worcestershire. I autographed a W.A. Poucher Book on Scotland for him.

The next time I saw him was in February 1973 when he came to an evening talk on 'Everest – the South West Face'. That was in Birmingham Town Hall. It was hard work for me to get there with the crew and all our equipment but this was as nothing compared to the problems it posed for Len. He first had to convince the surgeons at Oswestry Spinal Unit he could make it after being in hospital for seven months following a disastrous accident on the Matterhorn. The fall deprived him of the use of his limbs from the shoulders down.

He was in a wheelchair, dependent of friends for any move he had to make. He listened and lived every word of the presentation that night, as he had done on the earlier occasion. Len claims that this gave him the inspiration to declare war on his physical condition and to fight for restoration of as normal a life as possible.

It was the start of his own way of conquering his personal 'Everest'!

This book traces his story, from the days when his physical condition, as a child, gave cause for concern to his family because of his asthmatic tendencies. It takes us through his days as an athlete, fired with an ambition to prove he could run 50 miles a week on a training schedule that would eventually lead to him conquering the Matterhorn twice. The story of the fall and the brave actions of his Scottish companion, George Cloughley. The realisation by his wife Brenda of the magnitude of his injuries. The refusal of Len to accept a life of disability despite times of abject desolation.

His wonderful ability to talk, without notes, for hours at a time, on so many subjects, is, he says, a God given gift. It is a gift of which he makes full use and is largely what the book is about.

His ability to talk and inspire others!

It is never Len York who is the person with talent – it is always the person he is talking about. So many people have been inspired by him – not least the author of this book. This quality has always been with Len, both before and after his accident but Len maintains that anything inspirational he may transmit, comes from God himself.

A Long Way From Clent is not a book about climbing but the story of the fortitude and determination of a very special person.

Chris Bonington

Chapter One –

PINNACLE

"I will lift up mine eyes unto the hills. From whence cometh my help?"

For the millionth time Len York mouthed these words to himself and mentally climbed to the top of the snow covered peak at the centre of the mural on his bedroom wall. For the millionth time he was transported to 23rd July 1972. It was the second time in twelve months, that he stood at the top of the Matterhorn, on the very spot where Edward Whymper rested, on the 14th July 1865. He was elated, although concerned that it had taken until 1.30 p.m. to reach the top, almost the same time as Whymper's ill-fated day, one hundred and seven years before. Whymper was the first to climb the mountain successfully but he lost four members of his seven-man party on the way down.

Nothing had changed from the previous year. The peaks below him spread like an endless panorama of sugar covered points; coconut macaroons as far as his eyes could see. Mont Blanc, fifty miles distant, looked close enough to touch in the crystalline sharpness of the alpine air. The brilliant afternoon sunshine lit up the world just as effectively as it had on his earlier trip to the top.

Like Len, his companion, George Cloughley, needed time to recover his breath from the exertion of the climb. He stood, no more than six feet away, trying to absorb the beauty of the moment. He turned to shake hands and the friends clasped each other in a bear hug, cushioned by the thickness of their multi-layered, quilted clothes. This was the first time on the Matterhorn for George, although he was well experienced at climbing in his native Scotland, both in winter and summer. He was a formidably fit and careful athlete and at twenty-seven, he was seventeen years younger than Len. George felt good, but good as the feeling was, he knew it was not to be the most important happening in his life that year.

The climb had started before dawn under dark, clear skies whilst the snow and ice were crisp underfoot. The previous night had been spent in the scant comfort of the Hornli Hut below the Hornli ridge; a system of beds in tiers, reminiscent of mortuary drawers. Milk was not available at 2.30 a.m. at 10,700 feet, so breakfast consisted of Alpen, softened with orange juice. Len thought of his remonstration of a young colleague, the previous day, with a pang of sympathy.

The youthful climber had said mischievously, "We shall be OK. for breakfast – Len has some Alpen."

"Len will be OK. for breakfast!" Len had responded. The statement was accompanied by a penetrating stare into the young man's eyes.

The youth's embarrassment was clear. He lowered his eyes in a way that confirmed he appreciated the humour, whilst learning a lesson in the fundamentals of self-preservation. Each day in the mountains is tough and Len knew he was doing the young man a favour in pointing out his responsibility to himself. "You can't even be sure where you will be at breakfast time tomorrow – let alone where I shall be." The young man nodded and Len thought of the similar messages he had passed on to all the young cubs and scouts that he had cared for over the years at the camps he had organised in England.

Zermatt is traffic-free, other than for permanent residents so the party had abandoned the coach, completing the final part of the journey by shuttle. This entailed carrying all provisions that had been carefully packed in England. Tents, utensils, sleeping bags, spare clothing, cooking gear – all had to be humped in rucksack or carrier bags. It was no sumptuous outing. The total cost of the coach trip had been £27 for a two-week stay on the continent. The party were to be ferried, for this modest sum, to Grindelwald (Eiger), Zermatt (Matterhorn) and Chamonix (Mont Blanc). The reasonable cost had persuaded Len to take the trip that year.

He was to be reminded of the cost many times since.

From the crisp start in clear air the conditions worsened as the day progressed. The snow below the summit was slushy from the effects of the sun. The overhangs and icefields, familiar from the previous year, were less friendly. The snow was deeper and softer. Their progress was slow. The ice on the summit ridge was hard underfoot only because of the continuous cooling breeze that blew across the tops.

It had taken more than ten hours to reach the top ridge. The previous year, with Alan Plant and Bob Duncan, the pinnacle had been achieved by 8.30 a.m. Both years the weather had been fine, but the extra time taken illustrated just how different a challenge can be encountered, in what appeared to be similar conditions. It was clear that they should not delay their return. There was much time to make up, if they were to reach the Hornli hut before nightfall. They were tired from the exertions of the climb but George had proved his fitness over the past few days and they were now acclimatised to the height. Len had trained hard for years, road running up to fifty miles a week, climbing in Scotland and Wales and visiting the high Alps last year. Both felt equal to the demands that would be made on them.

Pointing his camera to the north-west, Len snapped two more views of France's highest mountain. The slides would be in sequence and his wife, Brenda, would enjoy putting them together to form a panoramic view of Mont Blanc for the scrap book, when he returned home to Halesowen. He turned again and bagged a good pose from his colleague, as George offered something from his gloved hand.

"Chocolate Len?" he enquired. Len needed no second bidding. They had not eaten since breakfast and there was little chance of anything else before reaching the refuge.

George pirouetted slowly, a full three hundred and sixty degrees, his twelve stone frame somewhat short of the grace required by a ballet dancer. He asked, "Did ever you see anything as beautiful as this, Len?"

"I take it you mean the view, not your ballet steps," Len smiled. "George, last year, when I stood here with Alan and Bob, we could find no words to describe it, until I made the comment that it was one of life's 'Magic' moments." He emphasised the word 'magic' by speaking it softly, as if slightly out of breath. "I still can't think of a better word to describe it."

They fell silent again as each man cherished the moment in his own way. A pinnacle of achievement that would live with them all through their lives. An inexplicable, inner contentment that stems partly from the physical effort, partly from the logistical challenge, but essentially from the beauty of the isolation of their surroundings.

For Len, he was with God, The Creator!

The moment of ecstacy ceased abruptly. As Len lifted the rucksack to his shoulder, his ice axe slid from its harness and started to career down the sheer East face. "Below!" he shouted instinctively by way of warning and they laughed together at the ludicrous implication that anyone would be making his way up that vertical slab. Mercifully, the axe wedged by its head in a small cleft, about twenty feet below them. There were several ice and snow bands to negotiate on the way down and they concluded that it was worth attempting a recovery.

George took the top rope and Len abseiled to the position where the axe was lodged. As he reached down to it, he was conscious of the thrill of total freedom, as he hung suspended, looking down at the duvet of alpine meadows clearly defined, many thousands of feet below. The world was in complete silence. This second moment of sheer magic was necessarily brief, soon to be broken by an occasional grunt and the brushing hiss of his clothes against the rock face as he reached the top again, the axe safely back in his hand.

Len raised his thumb to George, both as a gesture of thanks and confirmation that the detour had been successful. Synchronised in thought and movement, the two friends turned, in silence, to retrace their steps along the short summit ridge.

As they-slow marched, in line, Len thought of Zermatt. He had caught a momentary glimpse of it as he dangled from the rope a few minutes earlier and it set in train his thoughts to the jeweller's shop where he had called the day previously. He had ordered another necklace, similar to that which he had bought for Brenda the year before. This was to be presented to his Mom, who had so admired Brenda's. It was a gold-framed pendant, the centre of which carried a perfect replica of the Matterhorn.

Len was on holiday from his position of Chief Design Draughtsman for Kaye Alloy Castings at West Bromwich. He hoped that his designer's eye for detail had helped him choose the right piece of jewellery, just as it had always helped his ability to compose the photographic shots that he took with such care. He was to pick up his jewellery order the following day from Georges Muther's immaculate shop, in Zermatt, far below.

Len always preferred the climb down. Not because it was easier. Indeed, downhill can be more difficult – as Edward Whymper's famous party found in 1865. Len enjoyed drinking in the magnificent beauty continuously spread before him. The forecast was for cloud to form mist patches in late afternoon, so there was a dual spur for them to enjoy the views and complete the job.

They had made further slow progress and by 7.30 p.m. they reached one of the easier overhangs at about 12,000 feet. They paused and decided to finish the remaining chocolate and drink the water that had been collected as snow from the top of the mountain. They sat for a few precious minutes, each lost in his own thoughts. It occurred to Len that it was Sunday night. At this time he would normally be recessing down the aisle with the choir at St Hilda's Church, Warley Woods. Would they be singing his favourite hymn? "Love Divine, all loves excelling".

He was bought out of his reverie by George's rich, Scot's accent. "OK Len", he said, as if they had been discussing it, "We'll go down the same way as you did last year."

"Just let me fix this rope," shouted Len, who was picking away at the rock to secure a belay on the rope to which they were both attached. Whilst he concentrated on the job in hand there was a slight tug on the rope. George was about ten yards below him on the slope and quite close to the edge.

Len slid.

His crampons would not grip. He smashed the handle of his ice axe into the snow, into the scree, into anything, but he was sliding too fast. In what seemed to him, slow motion, he slithered past George and reached the edge. There was nothing but an eight thousand-foot drop. George yelled something but Len could not hear. He thought of Brenda, of his Mom, he shouted to God...........

He was in space and felt the air rushing past him with fearsome acceleration.

His head and left shoulder thudded against the rock face.

Chapter Two –

GEORGE

Instinctively, George dug his heels in hard, set his hips and held the rope in both hands, waiting for the tug that would launch him into space. He prayed to God to take care of Frances and his family and then stood, stupefied, as he realised that at the speed that Len had disappeared over the edge, he should have followed moments before. His hands were welded to the rope, his legs and hips were still rigid. He was petrified waiting for the fatal tug.

The silence was uncanny.

For fully ten seconds, George stood there not knowing what the hell had happened. He could only believe that Len had parted company with the rope that he was holding in his hands and had fallen thousands of feet to his death. What should he do? He traced the rope through his fingers and lay, face down, on the edge, looking into the void.   The rope was slack and had swung beneath the overhang, the end disappearing from sight. It seemed to be resting against the rock face below.

"My God what a hopeless situation!" he thought. If ever he needed a companion it was at that moment. He felt an inner panic that threatened to consume him if he did not pull himself together. He called into the silence surrounding him in the vain hope that another climber would be in the vicinity. He shouted again.....and again. The echoes of his call rumbled into the stomach of the enveloping silence. George was more lonely than at any time in his life. Was there no-one else left in the world?

Mechanically, he secured a belay. He threw the spare rope over the edge and tentatively started to abseil and scramble after the rope to recover the end of it which had obviously snagged somewhere below.......surely?

"Of course there won't be people on the mountain at this time of night," he told himself. "Those below will be holed up at the Hornli Hut and those above will be at the Solvay refuge. We could have stayed with them but for the fact that the hut was heaving with climbers when we looked in at the door about two hours earlier. They evidently felt that the more bodies in the hut that night, the warmer it would be, hence their enthusiasm to encourage us to stay. We decided it was more important to get down to Hornli where Frances, my fiancée was waiting. What on earth would she think if neither of us made it before 10 p.m.?"

It was these thoughts of Frances that brought George to his senses. He was tired, he would get very cold over the next few hours if he did not put in some work, and there was no one on hand to help him. He decided that the first thing to do was to establish what had happened to Len. Once he knew, he could decide on the next course of action. At this point the words of his instruction manual came to him – words he thought he had forgotten years ago – "Assess the situation before you do anything" they said to him. He kept repeating them over and over again as he got hold of a better position on the rock face. "Keep three points on the rock" the book kept repeating to him. He reached a narrow ledge and spotted a fault in the face which allowed him to drop a nut into the gap and fix another belay. This gave him the chance to lean hard back to scan the face in an effort to follow the track of the rope. To the left and above him he saw the rope sagging against the face and dropping at an angle of about sixty degrees, finally disappearing below him, around a pillar reminiscent of cenotaph corner in the Llanberis Pass.

George's mind started to focus again, "Could Len still be alive? No it's not possible." He was talking to himself again and at the same time he was unconsciously traversing the rock face by easing himself along the short ledge. The thought of what could await him at the end of the rope encouraged him to make haste and ignore his own safety as he was negotiating too great a stretch of rock face without fixing more pegs. Again he needed to stop and remind himself of the need to secure his own safety as a priority. He managed another fix and this enabled him to get to the edge of "Cenotaph Corner", to a position where he could peer round the rock, and see the back face.

An incongruous sight greeted him. About fifty feet away, Len's body was still attached to the rope, dangling above a fearsome drop. The rope had snagged on a deep "vee" that was cut into the rock. Len was suspended above a drop of thousands of feet. It was difficult to take stock from that distance and George continued his downward traverse until he was able to fix a final belay. He could reach out and touch Len's body from that position and mercifully found that there was a small ledge immediately behind Len's form. It was no more than six feet across and cut under the rock face to a depth of four or five feet. George was able to stand beneath the natural canopy formed below the rock and pull Len into an upright position. Then he managed to get another loop of rope around the middle of the limp form and tie the body to a series of rock spikes that stood like stalagmites in front of the recess.

There were no signs of life, but the position in which George found the body was nothing short of a miracle. Had the fall continued both he and Len would have been far below, waiting for the medics to pronounce them both officially dead. As it was, Len's forehead had sustained a wound on which the blood was already congealed. It had trickled down his unshaven face from what was a severe indentation to the head. He had fallen about 120 feet and George concluded that Len could not have influenced the position in which he was found, by any effort of his own. George was concerned about what other injuries may be masked by Len's crumpled clothes and hunched form. There was no pulse and no breathing but George removed Len's spectacles. One glass was smashed. He placed the good lens on the mouth of his injured friend for several seconds. When he lifted it to the failing light there was the faintest of occlusion. George's heart leaped. "My God you're still alive Len" he said to himself. Scarcely able to believe the evidence he went through the procedure again.

"You are alive you old bugger," he exclaimed. But there was still no other sign of life. He knew that he must get help from the Hornli hut as soon as possible.

When George got to "Cenotaph Corner" he turned to take a last look at Len. From that angle, with his limp posture and the blood from his head wound Len bore a striking resemblance to his friend Jesus, as he hung from the cross. "God Bless you Len," George prayed. He was on his way down, leaving the ropes as a marker for when, he imagined, he would return with a rescue party later.

It took ninety minutes for George to reach the sanctuary of the Hornli hut. His feelings, initially, were high at reaching the refuge but altitude and trauma can play harsh tricks on the psyche. He seemed quite incapable of spitting out the words that he had rehearsed silently to himself on the way down the mountain. Frances sat him down inside the hut and she was visibly shaken at the condition of her fiancée. "Where's Len?" she kept asking George but still he was unable to communicate through the gibberish that issued from his mouth. His body shook and he kept trying to raise himself from his chair to put his arms around his future wife. Help came in the form of a young Swiss who was 'host' at the hut for that night. He first of all calmed Frances and then turned to George. He offered him a drink of water and produced a phial of medicine from a cabinet on the wall. He assured Frances the drink would help to pacify the shock symptoms that George was displaying. Gradually George became calmer and slowly they were able to piece together what had happened.

"I am Victor," said the tall, thickset man. Now tell me, "Why are you so late on the mountain? Do you know where is your friend?"

George finished drinking the water and had taken the medicine. He wiped his mouth on the back of his left sleeve and spoke to the floor. "We are late because of the weather. The snow was too slushy to make good progress. Len is about two thousand feet up from here, near the ridge route, he fell on the east face side of the ridge!"

The guide seemed to have difficulty understanding George's Glaswegian accent and asked again. "Why did you not stay at Solvay if you were late?"

"Because Francis here, was waiting for us." He still spoke with his head slumped forward, holding his face in both hands.

"Can you say where again is your friend – so that I do not make a mistake when I go up there to help him."

George repeated exactly where he had left Len and the guide seemed reasonably happy that he could find him. As a parting shot he asked the Scot "Is he dead?"

This prompted George to look up sharply and he said to the guide, "Aye, he's no dead!"

Victor looked puzzled, walked over to another guide who came to greet them after a moment's conversation with Victor.

"Hello", he said. I am Lucky – Victor's brother. We are going to find your friend, but it is important to know if he is alive?

"Yes," said George. "He *is* alive." The accent on the middle word illustrated the frustration that had built up in him. He had worried himself sick in the last two hours and no-one would ever know how close to death he had come himself, climbing, scrambling, half-falling, cursing, in his haste to get down as quickly as possible. Here the guides didn't seem to want to get on with it. "Why are they asking so many daft bloody questions?" he asked Frances, his eyes becoming wild with worry for his friend.

Chapter Three

THOMAS AND MARIE-LOUISE

Next to the Hornli hut is the 'Belvedere' Hotel. A hotel at 10,700 feet catering for a specialist clientele of mountaineers and artists, together with people just in love with mountains. That night there chanced to be a member of staff named Thomas, who, apart from his cooking and management techniques, incorporated mountain guide and rescue skills into his busy itinerary. He was told of the accident by the brothers Imboden, two guides who had answered the initial call from the Hornli hut. It so happened that working in the Belvedere that night was Thomas's fiancée, Elizabeth, and her friend Marie-Louise. Marie-Louise had restricted knowledge of climbing techniques but she was a nurse and her immediate reaction to the news was that she would accompany Thomas on his climb to the injured man. The plan was to let the Imboden brothers (Victor and Lucky) have a short start ahead of them so that they could establish the position of the "body". Thomas would join them and they would attempt to bring the body down between them. In the unlikely event of him still being alive, then they would assess whether it was possible to bring him down.

"This is not the time for heroics" Thomas told Marie-Louise. "The dangers are great on the mountain at this time of night in the darkness. We know exactly where the body is on the face and I think we shall be able to get to it but it will take at least two hours to get up there. The chances are that the climber will be dead by then and it will be bitterly cold. What is the point in you risking all for a dead Englishman?"

He reckoned without the tenacity of the diminutive young woman and eventually was more concerned at losing time than arguing the point. Making sure she had the right tools for the job (crampons, warm clothes, light food supplies from the kitchen), he finally agreed.

The Imboden brothers passed Thomas as he went down to the Hornli Hut. The brothers asked him to talk to George who was showing signs of wanting to go back with the guides.

"My name is Thomas," he said to George. I am a guide and I shall go with the other two who have already spoken to you. First I must say that this is an operation that requires a detailed knowledge of the mountain, whatever happens. As senior guide, I cannot allow you to accompany us. You must stay in the hotel for the evening and recover from your exceptional tiredness."

George knew that this stranger was correct in his assessment of the situation and although he hated the idea of being left out, he knew it was common for someone under this degree of stress to be irrational. He looked at Francis and wearily nodded his head.

Thomas felt he was making progress and he said to George, "You have explained where Len is and we shall find him but it is important that we should know – Is he not dead?"

"Aye, he's no dead," said George. Thomas was confused as Victor had been earlier.

"George," he coaxed gently, It is important – is Len dead?"

It was one question too many for George. It took a second to summon up his strength. As loud as his tired body would allow him, he shouted, "He's no f...... well dead! Don't ya understand plain English?"

Suddenly, everyone in the hut understood perfectly – whatever their nationality.

Thomas pulled on his "gear", nodded to Marie-Louise, and the two of them stepped out of the hut, into a moonless, starlit night.

They walked to the climb and cleared the first pitch, which is rated 'difficult'. They then tackled the series of chimneys and ledges that punctuate the ridge climb on the East face. Thomas was pleased that progress was more or less on time. Although Marie-Louise did not have vast experience of climbing she was young and fit. With his own knowledge of the mountain and where there was a choice of route, he was able to guide her to the easier option.

After climbing for about one and a quarter hours they saw the lights of the Imbodens who were on their way back down and they waited a few minutes on a ledge to get the latest news from them.

"It is not worth us all staying on the mountain." stated Victor. "The climber is exactly where his friend described. He seems to be very badly injured, even if he is not dead. We cannot move him tonight because of the danger of further injuring the climber. What do you think Thomas – you are the boss."

Thomas agreed with them. He and Marie-Louise would stay with the climber and would arrange for a helicopter lift-off at first light. They worked out together a system of torchlight signals to confirm the arrangements between the Hornli Hut and the point where the body was strapped to the mountain. According to Victor, the hut was visible from there. Victor and Lucky were at the hut that night because they each had clients to take to the top of the mountain the following morning. There was precious little time for them to get back to the hut and get any sleep before they started out again with their clients at about 3 am. Their creed insists that in the mountains, if an injured climber needs help, the first duty of the Swiss Guide is to render assistance to the injured party, once he has secured his own client. As their clients were secure in the hut, they had done what they could for the injured man. Thomas and Marie-Louise wished their colleagues "safe journey" and left them to make their way back to the hut – about forty minutes below at the rate those two hardy individuals covered the distance. They were Forest Rangers in their 'other lives' and fitness was obligatory.

Within minutes of leaving the brothers, Thomas and Marie-Louise had reached the spot where George had left his ropes attached as a marker. The nurse could see from the reaction of Thomas that he was pleased at the accuracy of George's directions when he was so obviously distressed at the events of the night and was physically exhausted. Thomas decided that he would leave the route and trace the rope around the face at this point. Progress was slow as he belayed regularly and nursed his charge around the difficult ledges and precarious footholds. She was a brave girl to even contemplate the trip but she again proved how very capable and resourceful she was as she followed carefully every shouted instruction in the darkness. At times it was necessary for Thomas to disappear from view and Marie-Louise held her breath for what seemed an age until his reassuring voice shouted more instructions that helped her inch her way to "cenotaph corner". She eventually reached the corner and from there she caught the first glimpse of an obscure outline of a body against the rock.

"Come on" encouraged Thomas. "There is a small ledge behind the body and we shall be able to make use of it. George has done well. His friend Len is precisely where we expected him to be – even if George's language leaves something to be desired." They laughed together at that remark – the first time they had relaxed since the climb started. They both knew that it is unusual, in the panic that follows an incident, to have a clear guide given by anyone who has been involved in a rescue like this.

Thomas congratulated Marie-Louise on the way she had pulled herself up to this difficult spot, but he knew well that there was a long way to go yet! Thomas removed his rucksack and immediately produced from it a canister of oxygen.

Marie-Louise thought this was the point at which she should take charge. She searched Len's left wrist for any sign of a pulse but they both agreed that was wishful thinking. Len had been on his own, strapped to the face for five hours since George had left him.

There was no pulse!

He looked quite dead!

Thomas sighed with resignation at the thought that the journey had been almost a waste of time and he could look forward to a wait of about four and a half-hours to first light. It would be cold on the mountain that night and he dropped a survival bag around the hunched figure tied to the rock.

Marie-Louise picked up the oxygen bottle and eased the mask over Len's nose and mouth. Gently she fixed the straps behind his head. "I am going to give him five minutes only of this," she said with a new air of authority. Thomas smiled and mentally congratulated himself that the responsibility for the medical side of the operation had passed from him. "I'll time it for you" he said, directing the light from his helmet torch, to his wristwatch.

After four minutes or so there was still no sign of life but just as it was beginning to look a lost cause there was a splutter from beneath the mask. Len's body convulsed and then went limp again. The movement caused Marie-Louise's eyes to shine in the darkness and she breathed an involuntary "Wow", as though to communicate that it was the first bit of good news, although she did not allow herself too much enthusiasm at this stage. She adjusted the mask on his face and within seconds, he convulsed again. She took hold of his left hand and found confirmation in his wrist pulse that Len was alive. The effort had been worth it and they both allowed themselves a broad smile.

I think congratulations are in order", said Thomas. "I would not have given a half chance of finding him alive."

"I am not so sure he was alive when we arrived," she said quietly, "but he is now!" there was a certain triumphal note in her voice. This changed to a note of clipped resignation as she followed up with the statement "Work begins!"

Producing a bandage from the side pocket of the rucksack she gently wound it around the patient's head to protect the wound from infection, although it had been some hours since the collision with the rock face.

"We should leave him where he is" she said to Thomas. "His friend George did everything right – he is better strapped there than lying down - we could do more damage if we moved him. I think there are internal injuries and from the way he is slouched he could have serious damage to his spine fairly high up". Her early diagnosis was to prove chillingly accurate.

Whilst Marie-Louise spoke there was a sound from Len's mouth. A guttural clearing and then what sounded like "Bren ......Ben ....Bend", and his head lunged forward again, his body spent with the slight effort. His words unintelligible to the Swiss couple.

Thomas relaxed on the ledge and leaned back against the canopy. In minutes he had drifted into shallow sleep whilst the nurse continued to minister to her patient.

When Thomas woke he could not believe the continual stream of noise that was issuing from Len's mouth. Whether it was because Thomas had a limited understanding of English, or whether it was pure nonsense, he could not be sure, but it was a complete surprise to him and he was now re-assured that their journey had been vindicated.

"Shut the door – somebody's left the door open – it's so cold" Len rambled.

Marie-Louise was just as amused as Thomas at what was coming from Len's mouth. As if he were a baby, she coaxed and alternately, admonished him to encourage him to save his energy.

"Change the programme someone – this is an awful programme, change it over," he ranted.

His open mouth allowed her to feed him regularly with small pieces of mint-cake. He seemed quite capable of consuming the nourishing sweet whilst continuing to issue his unintelligible prattle. His nurse gently massaged his wrists, as she had been doing for the best part of two hours, trying to keep the faint pulse alive. She trusted that someone on board the helicopter would be able to administer an injection once the rescue operation was under way.

"Marie-Louise", said Thomas, when he had taken stock of the situation, "It will take us some time to get back down to the hut after the rescue services take him off. I think you should try to get to sleep for an hour while you have the chance."

"Not on your life," she replied with an extra sparkle in her eyes. "I have a patient here who is showing really encouraging signs of recovery. He needs all the help he can get 'til the helicopter arrives, and I shall continue to look after him. I am quite used to doing a full night shift." She smiled defiantly and Thomas knew that she too was now sure that she had made the right decision when she insisted on accompanying him.

He teased her, "Who the hell is in charge of this operation?" He knew her well enough to anticipate a pretty sharp response, so he took the opportunity to push his boots deep into his sleeping bag again and pulled it high over his head.

Her reply was muted – almost haughty.

"I am far too busy to deal with rhetorical questions at the moment!"

*   *   *   *   *

At first light, Marie-Louise was the only one of the three awake. Len had finally stopped his senseless prattle and drifted back into the unconscious whilst Thomas, an old hand in these situations, had allowed himself to fall into a deep sleep. He was saving his strength to tackle the climb down after the helicopter had left them. Marie-Louise shuddered involuntarily from the bitterly cold breeze attacking them from the East that morning. She wondered how long they would have to wait as the first flecks of pale light shafted pockets of a lighter glow on the nearby greyness of the hard rock. She was close enough to prod Thomas into grudging action. It took a few seconds for him to grasp the situation and he was glad that nothing was required of him immediately. He took off his helmet, allowing the cool air to ruffle through his thick dark hair. He rubbed his eyes. He smiled at the nurse and asked if she had managed to sleep at all. He was not surprised when she shook her head slowly from side to side, closing her eyes in resignation and smiling at the same time. "How is he?" asked Thomas. "When did he stop chattering?"

"About fifteen minutes ago," she replied. "He's dead beat, badly injured and unconscious. Apart from that, he's OK" They exchanged glances showing they both appreciated the humour of the remark but neither raised a smile, it would not have been appropriate.

"And how are you?" Thomas studied Marie-Louise's soft young face in the unflattering early light.

This time she allowed herself a smile that said more than words. It was clear that the opportunity to put her training to the test had sustained her and her patient, through the most difficult night of their lives. "I'm fine!"

Without realising it, they were both listening for the noise of the helicopter whilst they spoke to each other. In his experience, Thomas knew that it would take some minutes for the pilot, co-pilot and winch-man to check their equipment and scramble the machine. The craft had space for a doctor but it was unlikely that he would be with them. To get them airborne and cover the distance between them would take about fifteen minutes.

Thomas pressed his ear to the rock beside him. The noise would vibrate from the rock a few seconds before the helicopter appeared from whichever direction the approach would be made. It was clear that the machine would not be able to approach the rock-face too closely because of the overhang and the deep recess in the rock where they were positioned. He explained the situation to Marie-Louise who asked, "What will happen if they are unable to take him off at all?"

"It is probably the most difficult situation I have been involved in," he countered, "but it depends on the pilot. If it is Siggy Stangier he has a penchant for performing miracles. He does have a superb track record. He was involved in the first Eiger North Wall rescue and the Shilthorn cable car business. If he cannot do it, then it will be a very long job by hand with the full rescue team. I don't think Len has that sort of time left and the journey down for him would be horrendous. ....I can hear them .... they will be here in a few moments now. Come and stand away from the body!" he instructed, moving as far along the short ledge as he could.

"Why?" she countered.

"In a minute or two you will not be able to hear me for the noise.... it's all done by sign language with these chaps....and they need all the room we can give them to manoeuvre... come and push yourself into this corner with me!"

Before he had finished talking the helicopter was in view. It was below them and climbing up the face of the mountain looking for the exact spot. He wheeled away to the right and for a moment it seemed he had failed to locate them as he disappeared again from view. Seconds later the craft reappeared, about fifty feet above them and hovering.

The noise was frightening, particularly to Marie-Louise. Thomas had just said that they should not try to help and she knew now that they could not possibly do so while they were both forced to push their fingers between their helmet and their ears to cope with the pervasive cacophony that bounced back at them from all four sides.

The pilot closed in making his practice run. He found that he was not able to get near enough to pick up the body. The desperate danger of the situation suddenly gripped Marie-Louise, who was now convinced that a major catastrophe was about to take place before her. With eyes streaming she turned towards Thomas who opened his arms wide, turned up his hands and looked to the heavens, resigned to the fact that this noise had to be endured for a short time. The crew abandoned the attempt to get close enough to the face from this strategy and moved higher up the face, out of sight of the huddled figures on the ledge. They were so grateful for the relief this action bought, and after a moment realised that they could communicate again by shouting to each other.

"Is he going away?" Marie-Louise yelled at Thomas.

"No – he is repositioning.... listen .... he is getting back close into the face higher up. He will probably drop the winchman down to try and lift Len's body. The good news is that the pilot *is* Siggy." As he spoke the figure of a man appeared above them. He was waving to the pilot and alternately watching the aircraft and then the body. His arms worked overtime in exaggerated slow sweeps directing the operation inch by inch until he dangled no more than ten feet from the ledge and about two or three feet out from the overhang. It was clearly impossible for him to get to the ledge and as far as Marie-Louise could tell the operation was over so far as the helicopter was concerned. "He must be no more than ten feet from the face of the rock above the overhang," shouted Thomas .... "This is hellish dangerous."

The man hanging from the heavens was cocooned in a rope structure around his middle. He looked like an advertisement for a well known car tyre as he waved again to the pilot and started to swing slowly forwards with a movement of his body from the clip of the harness on the front of the webbing. He swung just underneath the overhang and then 'bounced' himself back again. His legs joined in on the next swing, projecting them as far forward as he could reach. The next swing took him back into view of the aircraft and his right arm went up in exaggerated salute to the pilot. Like a clock pendulum, he swung back and then forwards half a dozen times as though a child on a park swing. He was now swinging quite violently. Thomas took two steps forward to stand on the edge of the ledge, his rope taught between him and the belay he had secured when he and the nurse first reached the ledge.

At the next forward swing, Thomas held out his arms and the grateful winchman delivered a shout of triumph as they collapsed together on the narrow ledge.

Quickly recovering his equilibrium, the winchman delivered a series of tugs on the rope which Thomas and Marie-Louise took to be a form of communication best left to the initiated.

The winchman took control. In a military-style series of signs he made it known that they were to keep their distance whilst he quickly appraised the situation. He unwrapped his webbing to form a hammock on the floor of the overhang. He gestured Thomas to step forward and indicated that he would hold the body whilst Thomas was to unravel the ropes holding Len to the rock. In seconds the operation was over. Len lay on the hammock whilst the winchman took the weight of the rope suspended from the helicopter. He buckled together two snap fasteners to secure the hammock then indicated to Thomas that the body was to be pushed over the edge in the hammock. First the rope was tugged by him, then Thomas heaved the hammock over the edge and with it the winchman launched himself, clinging to the rope, only a foot or so above the body.

Simultaneously the helicopter moved away from the face and the two dangling figures moved perilously away. At the same time they were lifted towards the helicopter. As it moved away from them Thomas looked at Marie-Louise whose eyes were again filled with tears. This time tears of relief at the realisation of the miracle that they alone, in the whole wide world, had just witnessed. As they watched, the winchman climbed back into the safety of the aircraft, aided by the co-pilot. They continued to watch as the figures got smaller and smaller. They anticipated that the two men now in the helicopter would soon winch aboard the injured man but to their astonishment, the aircraft wheeled through ninety degrees, banked and moved away from the mountain.

The body of the injured climber was being carried, like a bag of sprouts, across the mountaintops he loved so much .... and he slept!

* * * * *

An overwhelming sense of redundancy overtook them in the silence that followed. It was some moments before they recovered themselves to the point where they collected their belongings and set about retracing their steps. Within minutes they encountered Victor again. He was with his client. They had started at 3 a.m. from the Hornli hut and had witnessed the rescue from "Cenotaph Corner". They waited to return down the mountain with Marie-Louise and Thomas ....the client had seen enough! Bearing in mind that several people lose their lives annually on the Matterhorn and having witnessed the rescue, albeit from a distance, the client had asked Victor to take him back down. He had lost heart completely in the climb!

Chapter Four –

BRENDA

Brenda normally accompanied Len on all his trips to the mountains. In past years she had particularly loved the trips to Scotland. The Claude Butler tandem was put in the Guard's van to Glasgow and they would cycle alongside Loch Lomond to the West Coast, north of Fort William. The short ferry across from Kyle of Lochalsh lent romantic excitement to the prospect of viewing the Cuillins from the beach at Elgol. The mountains seen across Loch Skavaig took on the appearance of a rugged skyline painted by the hand of a child. A series of sharp pointed peaks to challenge any range of mountains in the world. To view them late at night was to see them with a special 'aura' so far north on a late summer evening, almost as beautiful as the 'Midnight Sun' above the Arctic Circle.

The Cuillins were the range where Brenda achieved her most notable climb. It was Bank Holiday Monday 1960 when, assisted and coaxed by Len, against her better judgement, she got to the top of Sgurr Alasdair at the top of the range. She was in cycling shoes, as was Len. Footwear they would not dream of wearing on the ascent of mountains when they became more familiar with them in later years. The weather was perfect. They met another climbing couple, who encouraged Brenda up every inch of the 'stone chute'. Otherwise, Brenda still, to this day, does not think she would have made it.

Len's trip to the Alps was more than Brenda was prepared to do in the way of climbing and the opportunity to visit Jean was really too good to miss. In complete contrast to the Alps and the Highlands and Islands, her sister lived in the flatlands of Suffolk. A few days lounging on the glorious beaches in the area and a complete rest in the company of her beloved mother and sister was too good an opportunity to pass up. The first two days had been blissful in the sunshine of

Southwold. It was Monday lunchtime. They were sitting in the garden of Jean's home, enjoying a few joking remarks about how they were looking forward to a lunch without having to cater for menfolk with their particular fads and dislikes. Jean half raised an enquiring finger and her eyes looked heavenward as though these idiosyncrasies would quell the laughter whilst she listened intently – yes it was the phone – "Carry on talking," she said as she ran into the house. She could be heard animatedly chatting. Unexpectedly she returned, standing on the yard, beckoning with her finger raised. "Brenda" she called.

"Who is it – nobody knows I'm here".

"It's a Hazel Price. Is that your brother-in-law, Ray's sister?" "No – he doesn't have a sister." replied Brenda as she swept past Jean and into the hall.

Jean instinctively closed the door to preserve Brenda's privacy and rejoined her mother in the garden. It was one of those occasions when waiting for the outcome from a conversation lasting minutes, seemed an eternity.

Brenda replaced the ice-cold phone onto its cradle in the shaded hall of Jean's home. She hesitated for a moment and wondered if the conversation she had just had with the woman on the other end of the line had really taken place. This woman, this stranger, had just been talking to her about her husband – no she hadn't seen him but she had spoken to the doctors who had been attending him. Brenda was in deep shock. She had received news that her life would never be the same again. "Why am I not crying?" she asked herself. The question was almost rhetorical. She was already walking to the door to face the glare of sunlight, knowing that it was important to allow Jean and her mother space so that they could absorb with her the reality of the dreadful news.

Jean instinctively moved towards her sister to place a supportive arm beneath Brenda's elbow. Brenda's face was ashen, her slim figure slightly bent and high cheekbones drawn higher still with the strain of her secret. She did not look directly at her family. Her eyes were fixed to an imaginary point in the middle distance between her and the horizon. She reached for the table to take her weight. She pushed a chair into position and carefully lowered herself into it.

"It's bad news Brenda?" Jean interrogated her with a mixture of concern and dread.

"It seems to be very bad news," Brenda replied. "Len is in hospital in Berne, Switzerland," she said coldly, gazing still into the middle distance. Then she looked directly into Jean's eyes and said, "He has been taken off the Matterhorn by helicopter, after a fall."

"Perhaps it's not as bad as all that dear" reasoned Jean; "it is standard practice in the Alps to use a helicopter if someone has just broken an ankle, or an arm."

Brenda moved her head slowly and deliberately from side to side, her eyes still riveted to Jeans. "He has a broken neck....... he is unlikely to walk again....... and...... the surgeons have asked me to travel immediately to see him. They obviously fear the worst."

Her mother breathed a whispered "No, no, no!" while Jean could only divert her eyes from Brenda's piercing gaze. She rummaged in her handbag for a hanky. Brenda looked helplessly at both women in turn and asked imploringly "What do I do now?" She spread her elbows on the table in front of her and cradled her cheeks in her hands. As the comforting arms of both mother and sister closed around her shoulders, the floodgates suddenly opened for her, for Jean and their mother.

*   *   *   *   *

Hazel Price was from the consular section of the British Embassy in Berne. She had said that she would go immediately after the phone call to visit Len and when Brenda arrived at Berne, she would be there to meet her. She would accompany her to hospital, but first she would phone Brenda at 8 p.m. on that Monday evening with an update on her husband's condition.

Brenda did not have a passport and she had precious little money. The form filling and general running about, without the help of any mechanical transport, was all achieved by Jean with unstinting application, in the space of one afternoon. Brenda and her mother were to return home early the following morning.

Hazel Price phoned, as promised, on the stroke of 8 p.m. that evening. She had seen Len and astonishingly, had found that despite his serious injuries, he was in good heart and cheerful. Brenda explained that Len always gave that impression to the world, whatever difficulties he was facing, but she was pleased that he was sounding positive. Hazel also confirmed the booking for Brenda on a flight from Gatwick to Berne for Wednesday and told her that a hotel booking had been made in her name.

The helicopter crew had given Len's passport to George's girl friend, Frances, when the craft had arrived at the Hornli Hut. There the crew was able to transfer Len's still unconscious body to a stretcher which was then transported to the Hospital 'Inselspital', Berne, this time - inside the helicopter. A Doctor at the hut was able to give him an injection to help him survive the journey.

It was learned later that the authorities traced Brenda to her sister's home in Southwold by a mixture of good fortune and the local police being particularly tenacious. The consul had communicated Len's home address, obtained from his passport, to the Home Office in London. In turn, the police at Halesowen were contacted and they visited Len's home, only to find it unoccupied. The arrival of the police vehicle in the quiet residential area proved to be a sufficient lure to the neighbours to winkle them out of their houses. From one of the neighbours the address of Brenda's sister, Rita, was established. It was only a few hundred yards away. It was Rita who was able to give them Brenda's holiday address and phone number. This was then relayed to the Embassy in Berne via the Home Office and the rest was straightforward. They took care not to divulge the reason for their enquiries until the next of kin had been informed. All this had taken place within a few hours of Len being delivered to the hospital at Berne.

Chapter Five –

BERNE

The first flush of consciousness slowly began to ease Len out of his torpor. It was Monday 24th July. As he became aware of his eyelids opening, he saw the hazy, rounded shapes of the light fittings above him and concluded that he was in hospital. This was confirmed almost immediately by a young, white coated doctor who stood at his bedside, leaning forward over him.

"You are in Hospital Mr York; can you hear me?"

"Yes Doctor, and I can see you," Len confirmed.

"You have had an accident........." he began, but was cut off in midsentence by his patient.

"Doctor, let me tell it to you please, so that you will understand the full circumstances."

The doctor was completely taken off-guard by the patient's assurance.

"My friend and I were descending the Hornli Ridge on the Matterhorn on Sunday evening. At about 8 p.m., after a short rest, we started off again down the face when I was pulled from my stance."

The doctor was clearly shaken by his patient's ability to recall these circumstances so clearly and so quickly after recovering consciousness. Taking a step back from the bedside, his face twisted into a slightly amused smile.

"Honestly Doctor, I did not slip, I was pulled off, of that I am sure. Then I went hurtling down the East face until I hit my head against the rock and passed out."

The Doctor, by now, was speechless at the accuracy of the detail. He gave an audible chuckle as Len continued "It must be about 8 o'clock on Monday Morning now!"

Looking at his watch he smiled again and said, "Well, I will not argue with you for the sake of half an hour" (It was in fact 7.30 a.m.)

The doctor's face resumed an air of gravity. He explained to Len, gently and in very good English, that his injuries included a broken neck between the 6th and 7th vertebrae, sixteen stitches in a head wound, cuts requiring stitches in both legs and general bruising all over his body. He was very relieved that there was no obvious concussion and he told Len that he was very impressed with the calm manner in which he had listened to and accepted the news of these serious injuries. He went on to say that it was most unusual for anyone to withstand a fall of this nature on the Matterhorn and survive at all.

Len waited a moment and then said, "Doctor, before the accident I was fitter than I have ever been in my life. I had regularly been road running up to 50 miles most weeks and up to 70 miles a week at times. I had been doing this for some years and often included 30 miles a week cycling."

The doctor's reply brought the first smile to Len's blood encrusted lips when he said, "My God, the training you have been doing would have been enough to kill me – and yet here you are today – it has helped to save your life. Be sure that if you were less fit, you would not have survived the cold night on the mountain after sustaining such serious injuries."

"I have often wondered why I did train so hard," said Len; "God works in strange ways!"

Then, as if his injuries were not enough, the doctor produced an enormous safety-pin and proceeded to push the point of it into Len's legs, arms and body to prove that the broken neck had left him with no feeling in the majority of his body below neck level. Looking squarely at the doctor whilst this was going on, Len did not try to move any of his limbs, he did not flinch - he could not.

Putting down the safety pin, the doctor reassured his patient about the treatment he had received, whilst he had been in the unconscious. He explained that, fixed to Len's head, was a spring-loaded calliper. To keep it rigidly in position, the surgeons had drilled two small holes into his skull. Attached to this was a wire which ran over a pulley at the head of the bed. The wire retained weights totalling eighteen pounds. The purpose of this was to hold the neck rigid and prevent any further damage to the spinal chord. Despite the explanation of the seriousness of his condition, Len was sure that his fitness would not let him down. It would only be a short time before he would be up and running again.

He felt no pain, he felt almost that there was a contentment and relaxed assurance about him. He became aware of the presence of God. He was there with him. In the hospital watching over him. He would give Len the strength to combat the physical difficulties. Surely this was why he felt no pain. God was his shield. The words of one of his favourite hymns filled his mind. The hymn that he had remembered when on the mountain.

"Love divine all loves excelling"

His lips moved in prayer but no sound came out. He pictured himself at the altar of St Hilda's Church, Warley where he had been a member of the choir since he was seven years of age and wondered how long it would be before he would stand there again, lending his tenor voice to that beautiful hymn.

The doctor left the ward, to be replaced immediately by a nurse who enquired, "Mr York, would you like a cup of tea?"

"Like one?" he smiled again, "It has been 13 hours since my last drink. That was melted snow from the top of the Matterhorn. Yes please dear." Unusually, he asked her not to put sugar in it. All his life he had been addicted to weak, sweet tea but even at this early stage in his recovery he knew that the longer he remained immobile, the more weight he would put on and the more problems he would have to regain his fitness. The habit of a lifetime changed at that point, forever. Nurse held the beaker for him whilst he sucked the nectar through a straw.

As the morning advanced Len became aware of some warmth in his arms. The blood was obviously beginning to circulate again and, unbelievably he was able to raise his arms very slightly from the bed and everyone became intensely excited.

Len felt they were over reacting. He had no idea, even now, just how serious were his injuries.

Chapter Six –

HAZEL

Since regaining consciousness earlier in the day, Len had been concerned about his family.

How would Brenda be taking the news? How much did she know? What about Mom? She was so ill herself. How was she reacting? What of his three sisters, his two brothers, their families? How many of his friends back at home would know? Bob Duncan and Alan Plant, who had been to the top of the Matterhorn with him the previous year. The two Dons, Don Haskins and Don Saunders who had been with him on the Scotland trips over the past few years. West Bromwich Mountaineering Club, St Hilda's Church congregation, his staff at Kaye Alloy Castings, the wider family – so many cousins, uncles, aunts – the list was endless but he thought about them all. There was no shortage of time. For once in his life he had as long as he needed to think of them all; and think of them; he did.

Meanwhile the Swiss staff were so attentive to this Englishman who had no right to be there. If he did not appreciate the miracle that had preserved him, then the staff genuinely did. They moved expertly around the bedside taking samples of blood, conducting blood pressure tests, changing the drip-feed tubes that were gently supplying into his arm the fluids that were to supplement his own superb fitness and will to survive.

There had been phone calls from the "Daily Express" and "Reuter's News Agency" within two hours of regaining consciousness. With assistance from a passing nurse, who held the telephone to his ear, he was able to re-assure them that he was already on the mend and looking forward to his release from hospital, which he hoped would not be too long in the future. Very soon afterwards he heard the tones of a beautifully modulated female English voice approaching.

Hazel Price stood at his bedside and introduced herself to him. With his injuries and the intrusion of the frightening array of technological wizardry that was attached to him, Len felt that this delightful young lady would be frightened away in seconds. He was wrong! She proved over the next hour, to be a remarkably resilient person.

She encouraged and reassured him whilst gently shaking him out of the cocooned world he had thought himself into over the past few hours. Hazel was from the British Embassy in Berne. She had been in touch by phone with Brenda and had promised to phone her again that night to report on Len's condition. She was to meet his wife at the airport and would accompany her to Len's bedside on Wednesday, which was the first day she would be able to join him.

In the afternoon sunshine that streamed through the windows of the top floor suite of the Insel Hospital, Berne, the radiant picture that Hazel Price presented has often appeared to Len subsequently to remind him of the totally professional way that she handled the difficult job.

Len was now beginning to appreciate just how serious his situation was. If Brenda had been summoned from England and was in course of transit even at that moment, he must be in a worse condition than he had thought to date. "The one thing Brenda appreciates about me," thought Len, "is that I cannot stand anyone fussing about me." This was something that probably stemmed from his days when he was so sickly as a child.

He began to think more clearly from the time of Hazel Price's first visit.

After waking from unconsciousness, one of his first thoughts had been to wonder if he would be able to join his colleagues in Chamonix when they went over to the Mont Blanc Massif for the second week of the holiday. Now he was beginning to wonder if his remarks to the Daily Express and Reuters had been a little premature in suggesting that he would "soon be out and about." If he was so seriously injured why could he not feel any pain? He thought of the doctor earlier in the day who had stitched a wound in his leg without giving him any anaesthetic, and he had not felt a thing.

He thought about the lack of feeling in his arms. Arms that twelve hours before had been capable of lifting the weight of his entire body up rock faces with consummate ease. He thought of his legs. Legs that had carried him 50 miles in twelve hours with energy to spare. On six occasions he had organised and led the team in the walk from Kaye Alloy Castings, West Bromwich site, to Kaye Alloy Castings at the Presteigne site. Now those legs seemed to be separate from his body, although still joined.

What Len did not know was that the surgeon who was responsible for him had asked the Consulate in Berne to contact Brenda and ensure that she came over as soon as possible as Len was not expected to pull through. The surgeon had spoken to the Embassy early on Monday morning, soon after Len had been admitted to the hospital. He was in a poor state, despite his extraordinary fitness. Anyway, people do not have falls on the Matterhorn and survive!

Despite the dedication of the staff at Insel Hospital and the skill of the physiotherapist who was already beginning to get some reaction from his supine arms, Len was beginning to have some reservations. Doubts crept into his normally ultra positive personality. To relieve himself of the responsibilities of these thoughts his mind turned to yesterday when he stood at the top of the Matterhorn with George. The feelings of indescribable elation as they passed the Solvay Hut on the way down. They were relaxed and sure that the hard work and danger was behind them..........

The sunshine had disappeared from the suite; the soft evening light was beginning to make way for the first conscious night of complete darkness since the accident.

So ended Len's longest day.

Chapter Seven –

CONTACT

The following morning, Len lay in bed at the Insel Hospital, Berne, annoyed at himself that he had not been able to sleep for any length of time during the night. The hospital was full of the most recent technology; it was clinically clean and organised to a point that would have thrilled even the military. The balcony windows that looked over the immaculate Swiss scenery would have done credit to a leading hotel. The pale early morning light would normally have made his heart skip a beat as he anticipated the day before him, but it was Tuesday, the twenty-fifth of July 1972 and he was irritable. He lay, flat on his back, unable to turn, unable to move because his head was held in rigid callipers, the points of which were embedded in his skull. There was no pain below the level of the arms, as his spinal chord was broken between vertebrae 6 and 7, depriving him of all feeling below shoulder level, but there was pain where there was feeling. His hands, and in particular the tips of his fingers, felt like they did after snow-balling as a child. They were lacking normal circulation of blood and felt permanently "frozen". The difference was that there was no relief. As a child, after snowballing, normality was resumed after a few minutes of the "hot aches", but there was no relief that day. During the hours of darkness, in his semi-conscious state he was aware of frequent monitoring visits of the sister to his bedside. He had no words sufficient to thank her for her help in reducing the effects of the cramps that he was feeling. She seemed to know that with a supreme effort, he could raise his arm to the alarm just above his head. She also knew there was insufficient strength in his fingers to push the button.

He felt utterly helpless and bitterly frustrated that his limbs, such faithful servants when he had called on them to perform quite

unreasonable tasks of endurance in the past, were now denying him. "Will life always be like this?" he asked himself. "Will I be able to live this life with time passing so slowly. Why am I so uncomfortable?" During the night he had spoken out loud when he thought he was alone, "Why me God? Please help me..... please." It was though he was lying on a beach with alternate tides of unbearable pain and self-pity washing over him. His friends would, even then, be leaving their warm sleeping bags for another climb in these fantastic mountains, and but for one careless moment, he would be with them still ....
It really was the longest night!

The full light of day brought with it blessed relief in the form of a platoon of nurses bearing down on him. They were quite immaculate in their spotless white uniforms which contrasted with the blue worn by the sister in charge. They seemed to glide into the ward, without noise, in single file. They took up predetermined positions, three on either side of his bed. Without a word of command, they placed their arms beneath his unfeeling, helpless body whilst sister held his head. They linked arms beneath him and raised him whilst the other nurses washed his body from the back of his head down to his toes. This was a routine that would be repeated every day he was in the hospital. He saw the strain show on the face of the nurses holding his body above the bed sheets as they willed the washers to hurry and finish the job. It was, for them, a form of torture to be holding a heavy weight at arms length whilst being hampered by the edge of the bed pushing into their thighs and stomach. Len's heart filled with gratitude for their dedication and at the same time he loathed himself for putting them to such trouble.

The bed was freshly prepared with cool, clean, white sheets before the nursing staff were able to lower his grateful form onto the semi-starched surface. This proved to be the pattern each morning, but on that first morning he had been able to forget the pain in his arms and hands whilst he sympathised with the nurses at their discomfort. For a few seconds, in the clean feel of the sheets, he almost forgot his pain again but the next ordeal was already confronting him .... How he would cope with breakfast?

Eating was a torture. He coped with as much weak tea as the staff could provide, but had lost the ability to cough because of the loss of function down below. This meant he could not clear his throat and was living with the continual threat of choking. The staff understood this but it inhibited Len from eating other than soft, pulverised and minced items that had to be administered by the staff, a spoonful at a time. He hated being so dependent. He constantly told himself that it wasn't 'British' to be like this, being completely dependent on foreign people, in a foreign hospital. It took him a long time to appreciate that if he had to have such a disabling accident, he could not have been in a better place.

It seemed to Len that there was no let-up in the ordeals that he was having to overcome. Following breakfast he was waiting for the doctor again. He was waiting for some reassuring news but with shrinking confidence. When doctor arrived he had with him an entourage of seven or eight other pairs of eyes gazing stonily down at him, their faces full of compassion. Len waited for them to tell him he soon would be climbing again but he was disappointed. The doctor who had talked to him earlier said "Mr York, you are very lucky to be alive. We can only put your survival down to your incredible fitness. Taking into account your injuries you are in good condition physically and remarkably good condition mentally. Do keep up the good work."

That left him plenty to conjure with.

How did they know his mental state? Could they really know how scared he was? How lonely? How trapped into a situation from which there was no escape? The loss of the very mobility that had supported his independence all his life? Did they really understand all this, or was his indomitable cheerfulness fooling them? If so the strategy was working - must stay 'British'.

He had permitted himself this 'wallow' into his psyche for the first time since he recovered his consciousness. There were to be many such trips in the future with unlimited time at his disposal. Then he was yanked rudely back into the real world by the brisk appearance of the sister. Acting on doctor's instructions, she removed the drip feed from his arm. "I can take the tube away also now Mr York," she said. "Which tube?" he enquired. Without further discussion she pulled a tube from his nose, that had been passed through the alimentary canal directly into his stomach. It was disconcerting to him that he had not known of the existence of this tube. Whilst he was still grappling with this intrusion into his 'world', he was again being coaxed by two other nurses, "Preparing you for X-ray," as they put it.

After transferring him to a trolley he was pushed through what seemed to be miles of corridors, via several lifts, past dozens of interested faces and quizzical eyes. At last he arrived at what he could only think was the set for a science-fiction movie. Never, in his wildest dreams did he envisage that he would be positioned beneath so much futuristic machinery. It was all so beautifully styled; his designer's eye told him that it did not even look like machinery. There was not a sharp corner on any piece of the equipment and it looked as if it were ready for take-off any moment. He was left alone in this alien world for some minutes and again, he was beginning to have doubts and anxieties. He was lonely and insignificant......... helpless.

Eventually, the radiographer appeared. She explained what she was about to do whilst she manoeuvred the trolley beneath an electronic marvel with flashing lights. It emitted an eerie hum. She said there was nothing to be afraid of or apprehensive about. She and the rest of the radiography staff promptly donned heavy lead jackets and threw themselves behind a protective screen.

Len thought he was beginning to recover his sense of humour!

Back in his "own" bed, he appreciated the second visit of the physiotherapist. She was able to convince him that he still had hands and legs and it was worth persevering for any sign of feeling or movement in them. Len felt that the arms may have some slight feeling in the tips of the fingers but the legs still did not respond.

"Hello Len!" The cheerful voice of Hazel Price sang out as she glided along the suite toward him. This was a surprise to him; he did not expect so soon, a second visit from so important a person. She was as charming as she had been on the first occasion. She told Len of the difficulties encountered in tracking down Brenda and that she had spoken to her at home last evening to report on Len's condition as she had promised to do. She judged that Len was mentally more receptive today and reminded him of Brenda's trip to Southwold with her mother. Len felt quite foolish to admit that he had forgotten all about the holiday that Brenda had arranged with her mother, although he had sent a card from Grindelwald to the Southwold address only a few days before the accident. Was this the only lapse of memory, or were there other things he had forgotten?

Hazel confirmed that Brenda would be at home in Halesowen now and before she left, Len resolved in his mind that he would phone his wife that evening. Perhaps he could persuade her not to come. He was in good hands and he didn't feel too bad. It was a long journey. He knew she did not have a passport and it would take time and trouble to arrange. They may even let him out of hospital within a few days.........

Len still did not realise the extent of his injuries and the likely consequences. He was still not able to accept the truth. He would show them! He would soon have his body at peak fitness again. Just let him get at the gymnasium equipment.

The evening meal arrived. Whether the prospect of talking to Brenda spurred him on he was not sure, but he seemed to enjoy that meal better than any the hospital had provided to date. Perhaps the rapport between him and the nurse was improving.

She still had to spoon the food towards him and he gave the OK to put it into his mouth by opening his mouth or by smiling. A movement of his eyes in the direction of the teacup would indicate that he was ready for a drink. Nurse had to hold a glass tube to his mouth for him to suck the liquid. This was the person who expected to be released from hospital within days! He was no more able than a baby of a few weeks.

As soon as the meal was over, Len asked the nurse if he could make the phone call to his wife. She was delighted to be able to help and within minutes of clearing his food trolley from the room the bedside phone rang with a shrill, piercing note. It was the first time he had heard it ring and the intrusiveness disconcerted him. He could not answer it, of course, but nurse had anticipated this. She swept into the room, cradled the phone into an indentation in the pillow right next to his ear and glided out again to preserve his privacy. He felt like the central figure in some crazy ballet.

"Brenda..... Hello Brenda dear, it is good to hear your voice." He then launched into a monologue of breathtaking audacity. He told Brenda of his experiences of the last three days, speaking without a pause. The tirade was laced with as much jovial lightheartedness as he could muster, until he paused to take a breath.......".Len", said Brenda, seizing her one opportunity, "I will see you tomorrow!" Click, brrrrrrrr. The phone lay uselessly by his side and Len lay uselessly by the phone. He reflected on the mess he had made of that attempt to bridge the distance. He reflected on the trouble that he had caused to so many people for the sake of one careless moment on the mountain. Brenda's reaction on the phone told him more than all the doctors and nursing staff had managed to convey about the seriousness of his condition. He thought of all the frantic activity that was going on at home in England on his behalf. The work that would be being put in by his own family, his friends, particularly the amount of extra pressure put on Brenda's family ....and Brenda herself, what had he done to her world?

Len reminded himself that it was July, for whilst the pale evening sunlight still flooded through the windows he felt the world in his comfortable suite had suddenly taken on an autumnal chill. Another childish trait overtook him. As he lay turning over in his mind the totally unreal state of these sudden changes, an overwhelming need to shed tears took over. The more he tried to stifle the convulsions the more they came. Totally unable to feel them, he was equally unable to deal with them. The stiff upper lip disintegrated and he was powerless to hide his feelings in the bedclothes. He just hoped that no one would come in whilst he was so distressed. No one did.

No one saw him being totally human.

*   *   *   *   *

The brightness of daylight soon became entangled in the softness of approaching dark. As the light faded the cloak of blessed concealment masked the redness of his eyes. The darkness was pierced gently by the low-powered exit lights and through the ghostly shrouds that lurked in each corner of the suite, a disembodied voice spoke to him as though in answer to his private prayer. "Mr. York, if you are awake, your young sister, Margaret has been on the telephone asking about you. I told her if she rings again tomorrow she can talk with you. Goodnight!"

"Thankyou God" Len murmured into his sheets as the footsteps of the doctor softly drew away from him, "Thankyou Maggie." It was 'His' seal on a traumatic day for Len. Brenda was arriving tomorrow and the family at home were thinking about him and doing all they could from such a distance, to make him feel life was for living. The occasional sob was almost completely controlled now. The length of the day seemed to Len to be unreasonably long but then, every hour did consist of 3,600 seconds.

Chapter Eight –

DELAY

Brenda walked the last few yards of her journey home, up the familiar drive to her front door, with as much composure as battered confidence and weary limbs would allow. She and her mother wanted nothing more than to sink into the soft furnishings with a hot cup of tea. It was late afternoon on Tuesday 25th July 1972 and it seemed that half the population of England had other ideas. As her high-heeled shoes encountered the last few yards she inclined her head to one side to get a better line on what she thought she heard. She wasn't mistaken. It was the ring of the telephone. It was undoubtedly to do with Len so she quickly turned the key in the cylinder lock and swept up the phone in a single movement. She pulled her coat around her in a protective sweep, half fearing a message with worse news.

She stopped short when the voice at the other end of the phone was that of a local journalist. Brenda started to explain that she had only that moment closed the door after a long and tiring journey home following a sleepless night. There had been no opportunity in the previous six hours to update the position of her husband and his injuries, and could she phone him back when she had further news. Gentlemen of his ilk, however, are not to be put off. Skilfully he side-stepped the request and asked which hospital Len was in and how long was he expected to be there. Whilst she parried the shots, there was a knock at the front door. Thinking this would be a neighbour to help her get off this hook, Brenda opened the door whilst retaining the phone in hand. It was another man she did not know. He was brandishing a press card and telling her he would wait for her to finish her call. She closed the door in his face in a frustrated and vain hope that he would disappear. He did not. She opened the door again to him and he asked if he could take a photograph of her preparing to fly out to her husband's bedside. Not normally being of an aggressive nature she did not find it easy to put into words just how totally intrusive she considered the press to be when she had such a plethora of personal problems to solve. Mercifully, he seemed to glean from her reaction that the answer to his request was an emphatic "No!"...... and he left. That was only the start of the phone calls that night. Brenda needed to phone Len's mother, twin sisters Abbie and Beattie, young sister Margaret, brothers John and David at least. Of her own family, she must talk to her brother, Ray. Her mother and sisters had already been involved. Each of them had picked up sketchy news from the evening paper. They were concerned at Len's situation, and she felt obliged to pass on to each of them as much information as she had herself, qualifying this by carefully sifting her message to Len's mom, who was herself in the advanced stages of coping with leukaemia. Time was running short to allow Brenda to arrange for her trip the following day.

Without exception, help was offered, as is the case when such dire situations involve popular people. Brenda's brother, Ray, offered to accompany her to the station the following day and brother in law Derek volunteered to stay with her to London Airport. A hastily convened telephone conference between the family resulted in Len's brother in law, Jack turning up at Brenda's home that evening. He promised to be back at 8 a.m. the following day with £250 cash that he was collecting from the family in the meantime. In 1972, cash was not readily available. Brenda would be 'en route' in the morning before any of the banks were open. This was indeed 'Manna from Heaven'.

One of the incoming phone calls received during that chaotic evening was the call put in to Brenda by Len from the hospital. With all the pressures on her that evening she had surprised herself at her ability to deal so coolly with his plea.

When the door finally shut on the last visitor, Brenda and her mother were faced with unpacking from their aborted holiday at Southwold and repacking for the journey to Berne.

Brenda was filled with apprehension.

She had only been inside a plane once before, on a package holiday. The doctor had spoken in a severe tone earlier and the prospects for

Len were bleak. She would give anything not to have to go.

Sleep did not come easily that night, in spite of all the love of the families that surrounded her.

*　　*　　*　　*　　*

Brenda's mother also had difficulty with her sleeping. She was up at dawn, making tea for them both. They sat for a few minutes on the side of the bed, sipping the early morning nectar, collecting their thoughts and organising the day in their minds but they both knew that the day would not run true to any plan – there was far too much activity.

By 8 a.m. when Jack arrived with £250 in cash they already had completed what would have counted for a full days work on any other day. What a Godsend Jack was. So reliable ....such a worker. He had covered miles collecting the cash from the family and delivered it spot on time. A remarkable piece of co-ordination. What a boon at such a time·to have access to his ordered and logical mind.

Brenda was beginning to feel that she was taking part in a well-choreographed play when Ray and Derek arrived with precision timing and she was away from the house with a minimum of fuss. She had purposely not listened to the news that morning for fear that there would be reference to her husband's accident. Mercifully, people who knew her had refrained from calling her on the phone so she was able to start the journey without hindrance from that direction.   She had left mom in charge of that side of the operation and Ray would pick her up after delivering his charges to the station.

From the moment she stepped out to get into the car, she felt that she was the focal point of everyone's gaze. She knew that some of the neighbours would be watching as she left the house. Not unkindly –they were in sympathy with her but not quite sure how to approach her in these difficult circumstances. One waved openly to her and mouthed "Good Luck" from behind the curtained window. That hadn't happened since her wedding day she thought to herself, as she opened the door of the car.

On the journey into town the newsboards shouted to her from the pavements outside the shops, "Climber injured on Matterhorn,"

"Local man in fall," "West Bromwich Climber – Serious". Len's connection with West Bromwich was from his membership of the West Bromwich Climbing Club and a passion since childhood for "The Albion".

New St, Birmingham served to provide two points of contact that morning. It was provident of Thomas Cook to site their travel shop so close to the station. This enabled Brenda to pick up traveller's cheques and Swiss currency – but not until she had waited with her male companions until opening time at 9 a.m. She still felt that she was on a stage, the focal point of all gazes from folks passing by. The news hoardings were telling them of her husband's condition and they would suspect she was the wife on her way to his bedside. They would tell from her pallor, her wrinkled brow, and her sense of complete disorientation... it must have been communicating to their enquiring minds as they hurried past. The station exuded the usual early morning cacophony born of frenetic activity, impatient traffic. Tannoy announcements drowned in the bustle. Yet she perceived a sense of organisation in this chaos. How she would have hated being part of this scene as a regular commuter to the city.

She enjoyed it as the shopping Mecca that she knew on Saturdays. Brother-in-law Derek was the only person that day to rise above the hubbub. In no time he had shepherded Brenda through the travel agents, past the serried lines of patient black taxis on the ranks outside the main entrance to the station, and found them both a seat on the London train. Two suitcases carefully stowed where they could be observed. The train was full of businessmen with briefcases, all wearing a grey-suited uniform of boredom. Once the train had moved its wheels forward no more than one revolution, their faces relaxed, relieved that it had started on time and they would make their appointments in the bigger city. Each countenance hidden from view for the next two hours, enclosed in the world of Fleet Street claptrap. How glad she was that she had had the strength to rebut the journalist who wanted to take her picture. There would have been no hiding place for her with that emblazoned across the front pages of the "Post".

She looked out across the green fields of Warwickshire as the train worked hard to reach its optimum journey speed. Brenda was conscious of the tight time-schedule, if they were to reach Gatwick in time for the flight at 1 o'clock. She did not read, she could not eat, and she spoke little to Derek on the journey but was comforted by his mere presence. A kindred spirit in a sea of uncertainty that threatened to drown her. Her thoughts were trying hard to come to terms with her husband's condition, which, from the two phone calls, seemed perilous. He did not appreciate the threat to his very existence that the fall had presented. He sounded so much like his "old self" on the phone that she could feel in her bones the tremendous effort he had made to achieve the illusion. "Yes! that's Len," she thought and was surprised as a smile contorted the corners of her mouth. How well she knew that indomitable spirit of his. The fearsome drive that powered him through his self-set goals and ambition, to show the world that his once suspect frame would win. Last night's phone call was so typical of him. She at home fearing the worst from the paucity of information that had reached her. Afraid to pick up the phone; even if she had the time; for fear that she would upset him, or make the situation worse for the hospital staff who were trying to save his life. And there he was – on the other end of a phone, sounding for all the world exactly as he did the day he left the house to join the coach for his trip to the Alps. "Don't bother to come" indeed – what did he think she would do then? Continue her holiday with her family? Spend the evening at the Coliseum, a local dance hall that was among their favourites a few years earlier? Wheel the Claude Butler tandem out of the garage that they had travelled many thousands of miles on to Scotland and the Alps and do a few miles on her own? Take a party of cubs and scouts on a camping expedition as they had done so often? Then she did allow herself a smile - she knew that, if he survived, he would appreciate a recantation of her thoughts with his brilliantly honed sense of humour. How dare he think she wouldn't make the effort to get to his bedside. How dare he think that it was an expensive thing to do? He hadn't said as much on the phone but she knew he would be thinking so. Yes she knew him! How is it this man could still stir her emotions to a fever pitch of indignation, with a few well-meaning words? After 20 years of marriage! Indignation wasn't a normal trait of her nature, was it?

"Of course," she resolved, "It's because I still love you Len!" She jolted herself out of her reverie by almost saying the words out loud to the crowded compartment. She looked self-consciously through her careful eye make-up but she need not have concerned herself. Newspapers still held the stage. Sensing that Brenda needed to wrap herself in her own thoughts, Derek had hidden himself behind the sports page. Perhaps this would conceal his concern about the tightness of their schedule.

At Gatwick, they ran to the flight booking-in desk, whisked through the formalities. Derek was bidden farewell and Brenda went through the passport check still at the double, when the airport official called her back.

"Where are you going?" he shouted to her, walking towards her as she wheeled round to face him.

"Switzerland" she retorted, her face flushed with agitation.

"No you're not," he said, pointing up to the sky – "Not on that plane!"

This was just about the worst scenario. She would have to wait twenty-four hours for the next plane. The official arranged for an announcement over the public address system for Derek. He had waited – hoping to see the plane in the sky – but with Brenda on it! He was able to meet up with Brenda and they arranged for rooms at the hotel so that he could see her onto the plane next day.

i) *Len, Chief Draughtsman at Kaye Alloy Castings Ltd., West Bromwich.*

ii) *Len's great grandad, John Drew. He was pit manager at the Jubilee Pit on the West Bromwich/Handsworth border. The photograph is one of the earliest to be taken down a mine – about 1900. It has been used extensively by the Black Country Museum, which has exhibited it at the entrance to the pit in the museum.*

iii) *Len's grandad, John Drew (Junior) who was working at the coalface by the light of a tallow candle. An early picture of a pit man – taken around 1900 at Jubilee Colliery, West Bromwich.*

1969.

iv) *Len, in earlier days when his fitness runs often exceeded 50 miles a week.*

v) *Len and Brenda – pictured in front of the Matterhorn in 1995.*

vi) *Len in his wheelchair in front of the Matterhorn in 1995.*

vii) *A shot of helicopter HB XDA as it was taking off in 1993 – the 21st anniversary of his fall. Len says he had to pay the pilot extra money to get him to stop the blades whilst they were in the formation of "Y" for York!*

viii) *Len in Highland regalia – prompted by his friends Kathy and Ewan Robertson, on a visit to Broadford, Isle of Skye, on 3rd June 1993.*

ix) *20th July 1992. Len studies the climb from the same helicopter that plucked him from the face twenty years earlier. Viewing the shot through a magnifying glass will pick out the Solvay Hut (about half way between the snow shoulder and the bottom of the picture). Len says he may never have attempted the climb if he had seen it from the helicopter beforehand.*

x) *A collage of friends at The English Church, Zermatt.*

xi) *Brenda climbs on fixed ropes above the Hornli Hut – July 1992. Her smile belies the effort she had to put in to reach this spot.*

xii) *A composite picture taken of Len and Alan Plant on the Matterhorn in 1971.*

xiii) *July 1971. Len and Bob Duncan with an unknown Swiss guide, on the precipitous ledge outside the Solvay Hut at a height of 13,200 feet.*

Chapter Nine –

MARGARET

Wednesday the 26th July 1972 was another day of long sunshine. Len knew that Brenda would not come that day and he decided to have as much sleep as he could, so that he would present his best possible face to Brenda when she arrived the following day.

Or so he thought!

When his sister Margaret had spoken to the hospital doctor the night previously, she was still grappling with the fact that her big brother had suffered what sounded to be a fairly serious fall. Len, who was responsible for encouraging her to do a few testing walks herself in the past and who had introduced her to Snowdonia and the Glyders. This indestructible man who spent his life, when apart from the family and church, maintaining a level of fitness that most people could not even imagine, had fallen on the Matterhorn? Had he not been playing with her two-year-old daughter, Julie, two days before going on that holiday? Had they not received a card from him only yesterday, describing with his customary level of unbridled enthusiasm, his climb on the Eiger and how much he was looking forward to his second visit to Zermatt? Was this really the same man that the doctor (who sounded so pleasant and friendly) was talking about? What did he mean, "I am afraid he may never walk again?" That's not Len .... he's my brother........ It can't be Len.

She had put down the phone in a condition of some shock and still felt sick in the stomach the following day, when she spoke first to the doctor and then was handed over to Len.

"Hello Mag" he said, his voice ringing with his usual strong tenor, "How are you?"

How am I, she thought to herself. She wanted to cry but knew that she mustn't.

She wanted to shout with relief at hearing him sounding just like his old confident self, but she mustn't. What are the right words to say at moments like this?

"I'm OK" she said, "but that's not important – how are you is more the point?" Then, taking the line from her brother, she permitted herself a false degree of levity. "You sound as if you have stumbled on a walk up Clent rather than down a mountain face in Switzerland."

She told him how wonderful it was to hear him, how loud and clear was the line for someone so far away. "How was the weather?" Anything to avoid having to touch on the shattering news that she had received from doctor last night. "Did he know how serious the injuries?" she wondered. "Surely the doctor was mistaken." But he wasn't mistaken; Len certainly knew the extent of his injuries. He had told her that his neck was broken, that his spine was damaged and that his head was cut. She did not know about the discomfort that he was getting from the head and body harness nor the humiliation he felt at the extent of the care and manhandling. Pervasive feelings of guilt were beginning to enter his thoughts. Why should he be causing so many people so much work, why should so many people be worrying about him?

Margaret put down the phone and relayed as much as she could to husband Brian. Would he be an angel and phone Mom and her twin sisters, Abbie and Beattie? She could only just squeeze the request out as the emotional top lip quivered. Her mouth pressed involuntarily closed as she tried to suppress the feelings that would finally out ....she knew. .... as she climbed the stairs

* * * * *

Hazel Price had called to see him again that morning. It fell to her to tell Len that Brenda would not be able to get to him that day. To soften the blow she had bought a dozen red roses and he was grateful for her words of encouragement. She was a round peg in a round hole if ever Len had met one. So thoughtful. So encouraging, So competent. She would never know how much those early visits of hers had helped him keep his sanity, at a time when things were looking so dark for him. What astonished Len was the level of interest that was being shown by the few people surrounding him and the thousands, it seemed, outside the hospital and far away, who were also concerned. Late in the afternoon, after he had eaten his soft-fruit offering and enjoyed his weak cup of tea, he dozed successfully. He had told the nurse who had helped with his food that he was "Still feeling well in the parts that are working". "Unfortunately", he continued, "there don't seem to be many parts that are working". The desperation of his true situation was gradually beginning to insinuate itself into his thoughts. He mentally chased them away but only for a short-lived respite. They had a habit of returning. Rekindling the apprehension.

His twilight world in the twilight of the day at Berne was interrupted ever so gently that evening when his eyes partly opened to reveal a new figure above his bed looking down at him. He was dreaming.............. He had to be dreaming. The evening sun shone low through the windows on the west wall and his waking eyes were clouded. A face surrounded by a halo created an ambience like nothing he had ever experienced. His years of religious faith and belief had not prepared him for this. He was at the Gates of Heaven. The Lord had called him.

So this was Heaven.

It wasn't Gabriel.

It was female, this kindly face full of serenity.

The Virgin Mary?

His Anglican learning did not preclude her from this situation then?

The Angel of Berne, in a voice so quiet and small, whispered: "Mr York, I hope you don't mind me coming to see you."

She put her hands to her face and lifted the white lace from her head. The sun streaming through it had created the illusion of a halo. It was the largest brim Len had ever seen on a hat!

His eyes were wide open now but he needed a moment or so to recover his composure.

Sensing his surprise, the figure spoke to him again. "My name is Ruth Brozy – I read in the paper about your accident and felt I must come." The English was flawless. As if she had a divine passage directly into his thoughts she said, "My mother was English, although my nationality is Swiss. I came to the hospital many times to see my mother but today I have come to tell you that God will take care of you and that you will get better." The beautifully 'English' choice of words, thrilled Len.

Since the accident, this was the first time anyone had spoken to him, about "getting better". Given his state of half-sleep and the half-light in the ward at the moment of contact, coupled with his desperate need for some comfort he could have been forgiven for mistaking her for a messenger from heaven. She proved, subsequently to be a person who easily measured up to that early promise in the eyes of Len and Brenda. She would visit him regularly, she said, whilst Len remained in Berne. How significant that the first visit should happen on the day when he was so low in spirit. The day when Brenda should have visited him, but was forced to delay for what seemed an interminable duration – a full day. For Len, this was the hand of God at work. The Lord had indeed, sent an angel to him.

Ruth Brozy had a Swiss father and an English mother and lived in Berne. She was probably sixty-five to seventy years of age, but age is notoriously difficult to assess. Deeply imbued with the Roman Catholic faith, she believed God would take care of Len. That Len's faith was wedded to the Church of England made no difference to her sincere support and they found a deep strength together. She needed to see him and help him in his solitude. She was not aware who might be arranging to see him. She did not know if he had any family. It was of no consequence to her. She had been called to this Englishman's bedside and could help him. She knew. She would visit him daily until she was well enough to go home. She had told him so.

By this time, Len's mind was beginning to become more receptive to his situation. His nature would not allow him to accept that he was in an impossible condition so far as walking and recovery were concerned. Anyway he was British, wasn't he? Couldn't let the team down in front of these foreigners, could he! The stiff upper lip was sagging just a little. Hearing the soft, confidential encouragement of Miss Brozy, combined with Brenda's guarded, hesitant words on the phone and the careful words of the hospital staff, the message was beginning to get through. The fact that Brenda had not yet arrived, there had not been time for messages and letters from home to get to him, apart from the call from Maggie that he would treasure for the rest of his life. The rest of his life? How long will that be? He could not move but he was beginning to think......

The words of the famous poem by Rupert Brooke continually recurred to him:

> "If I should die, think only this of me:
> That there's some corner of a foreign field
> That is forever England. There shall be
> In that rich earth a richer dust concealed; ...."

At that point his memory, the best part of him that was working, let him down. He could not recall the next line, but the first four lines were beginning to haunt him. If only there were a tune that had been set to these words, he would have remembered them as well as he remembered the hymns that he had learnt from childhood.

Ruth Brozy's faith was by far the stronger! Thank God!

Chapter Ten –

CLENT

Brenda was losing track of the days. Was it really Thursday? Derek had left her at the airport at 11 a.m. and at last she was *en-route* via Danair to Berne. It was her first flight to a mainland country on the continent, although she had been to Mallorca on a packaged holiday. She had toured the continent with Len several times in the past but each time they had crossed the channel by ferry and then cycled. What a pity, she thought, that the first time in a plane without a travelling companion, it should be on a mission of half mercy\ half dread at what awaited her at the end of the flight. She was not surprised that she did not feel up to reading. Although there had been plenty of time for sleep since arriving at the airport the day previously, it had come only in short, fitful bursts. Her mind kept returning to Len's condition, to what they had achieved together and the very special relationship they had enjoyed, in the open-air environment Len had encouraged her to share with him.

Leaning back into the relative comfort of the reclining seat she allowed her mind to drift as the plane sped smoothly through the stratosphere. She was trying to come to terms with the sure knowledge that her life would never be the same again. What of Len? He had not only the physical problems to deal with but also the mental and psychological ones that would be so much worse for a man of his outlook. Much of what he lived for had dissolved in the snows of the Matterhorn in seconds. That was important – their own relationship – that was something she knew she could maintain, no matter what. He had the advantage of a loving family of brothers and sisters and an ailing but adoring mother. A mother who loved Len as she loved all her progeny, and the wider family and all their offspring. A mother who was responsible for the early learning, the careful guiding and the Christian approach to life with which Len was deeply imbued.

Would the fall shake the faith?

She thought of her Dad and her own mother, her sisters and brother and wondered what affect all this was to have on them and their relationships with her and Len. First signs had been good. They had been wonderfully helpful. She remembered as a child climbing on Dad's knee and asking him to sing. Invariably it would be a few choruses of "Home on the Range", principally because she had asked for that tune. She remembered the less happy side of growing up when the girls of the family would be chastised for all the normal things for which girls were chastised in those early days. Dad played the violin and the piano. He used to play at his own mother's house in Causeway Green Road. Granny Davies's house. All the family had bikes then and on bank holidays, Dad would take them all cycling to Clent. The hills at Clent were probably her first introduction to the "great outdoors" that was destined to play such a big part in her life. Dad the toolmaker, making tools for the booming car industry after the war. Then there was the other side of Dad – the one that appeared when he had one of his epileptic bouts – how cantankerous he was at times – the arguments. How Sister Jean, being the eldest girl in the family, paved the way for Rita and Brenda by bearing the brunt of Dad's temper. It was comparatively peaceful by the time Brenda wanted to spread her wings. Tough at times it was with little money and a life regimented by school and by Dad, but what a wonderful grounding for the disciplines of life. Living cheek by jowl in the little council house at Warley. Mother taking all things in her stride. What a paragon she was to deal with Dad at his very worst moments, with no sign of argument. Never a bad word for anyone. Would that Brenda herself could be her mother. Perhaps her example would serve to help her from now on.

Her thoughts returned to the immediate prospect of meeting Len. With another hour of the flight before her, she thought back to their first meeting. The youth club dance at St Katherine's Church. Fifteen years old at the time, she was dazzled by this tall, athletic fellow, with flaming red hair. Five years her senior, he asked her to dance....... or did she ask him in the 'ladies invitation'? She wasn't sure. It didn't matter. What a talker he was. What an active person. He had done it all – scouts, walking, climbing, running, cycling, cricket, soccer, "In goal most of the time," he told her, "No-one else was daft enough to take that job on."

What a willing talker.

What a willing listener.

She soon found herself joining the youth club that he ran – the one in Rathbone Road. Well, he appeared to run it, although she didn't think that he was the official leader. That was Len. That still is Len, she thought. Even as recently as their last phone call, he was talking her out of going to Berne to join him. She knew him well enough now to sense the motivation – he would be worried that he was putting her to more trouble than his situation demanded and there was, of course, the question of the expense. He did not realise the seriousness of his condition and he was not capable at that time of thinking straight with the after effects of the shock he had suffered. That is why, unusually for her, she asserted herself; told him what she was doing – and then virtually hung up on him. That was one way to "shut him up" when he was not being rational.

Was that her mom coming out in her, she wondered, or was it Dad?

Why was it that at times like this when there was so much resting on her slender shoulders, her mind dwelt on long-gone days. It always happened when there was time to think. "How could all this help Len?" she thought, as she wrestled to bring her thoughts back to earth. "Back to Earth?" she quizzed herself – "At 30,000 feet?" She gazed through the window of the plane and saw nothing.

She was, she thought, such *a long way from Clent!*

Chapter Eleven –

STRANGERS MEET

It seemed ages since the plane touched down at Berne before Brenda walked uncertainly down the aircraft steps and onto the tarmac. Not being familiar with the sophisticated ways of air travellers, the composure and relaxed talk of her travelling companions did nothing for her. She could not help feeling awkward. The others were in couples, or travelling with companions who were obviously well aquainted, she knew from the familiar chuckles and comments they exchanged. At the bottom of the steps, the hostess from the plane stood with a good looking, dark haired woman in her thirties. Brenda noticed the neatness of the woman's suit and was taken completely by surprise when the handsome face flexed into a warm smile and she enquired "Brenda York?"

Hazel Price was as efficient in person as the first impression she had made when speaking on the phone. Brenda took an instant liking to her. "Let me take your bag so that you can hand your passport over when you get to the first desk" she said, unobtrusively educating her charge in the form for these occasions. "Then we shall have a short wait before your luggage will be ready to pick up and then I will get you to the hotel. What have you had to eat?"

Brenda explained that the food on the plane had been hardly touched and that she wasn't of a mind to eat really – and hadn't been since the news. "Understood" said Hazel with a slight narrowing of the eyes, that said more by way of implicit message than her words.

They waited for the luggage to arrive on the carousel. Each spoke in carefully measured tones. "Do you know how Len is today?" enquired Brenda. "Yes, I called to see him this morning before coming on to meet you. He's......I suppose........a bit mixed. His doctors say he is a miracle. They say that people do not fall on the Matterhorn and survive, but he has, and he is keeping them all amused and on their toes. He is in a form of neck and body harness that restrict his movements considerably but he is delighting them in his efforts to eat and exercise his hands and any part of him that he can manipulate. Quite a hero in his way," she said, as if this should be news to Brenda. It wasn't. Brenda would be surprised, if the doctors had said anything different, knowing of her husband's propensity to confound all the experts, all the time. "He must be so wonderfully fit," said Hazel, "Otherwise, they are convinced he would not have survived the fall". Brenda remembered the same words had been said of Duncan Edwards in the tragic days following the Munich Air disaster and how hard he had fought for life. She remembered how Len had followed the England and Manchester United star's progress hourly all those years ago. Duncan had been born in Dudley. Len was passionately welded to football and the 'Black Country' and she remembered he shed tears when news of the man's death was broadcast. She hoped to God that the consequences would not be the same. "How long before we get to the hospital?" she asked Hazel.

Hazel asked her to settle herself at the hotel first. Whilst she had the advantage of the embassy car to ferry her about, Brenda might make full use of it and she could then be taken on to the hospital later.

It was early evening when she eventually arrived at the Insel Hospital, Berne. Hazel had satisfied herself that Len was available and that the doctors had finished their rounds for the next hour or so. She walked to the ward with Brenda, pushed open the door, and melted into the background as Brenda walked hesitantly toward the enormous bed with the belts and pulley arrangements. It looked like a shipyard repair bay! Her husband lay in the prone position, with what seemed to be a grotesquely extravagant head harness. His face was positioned so that he looked up toward the ceiling. He was so still, she thought he was sleeping but through her misted eyes as she walked toward the bed, she realised that his head was rigid. Her husband forced round his eyes in their sockets to a crazy angle so that he could see her as early as possible. He recognised her fully seconds before she recognised him. She halted one or two steps from the bed and he grinned at her in his inimitable way, every muscle in his face alight with pleasured anticipation. "Hello Brenda, you've come to see the old man then.....the old crock". Her face creased into a smile as she held back the floodgates that threatened to burst. "You are a sight for sore eyes, and feet and arms and legs," he said as she bent low over him to smother his words with her mouth. "What have you done to yourself Len? How do you feel now? Which part hurts most? What am I allowed to touch?"

"You can touch anything – I'm not so sure I shall feel it though. No – I can only feel above my neck at present. My hands are beginning to respond to exercises and the feeling seems to be coming back into the ends of my fingers. I shall be OK now you have arrived!"

Later that evening Dr.Lanzrein called on his rounds and spoke to Len for a few minutes before asking Brenda to call at his office along the corridor whilst the nursing staff prepared her husband for the night. He was so gentle and patient with her as he explained the extent of Len's injuries and how he saw them being treated when Len returned to England. He apologised to her for insisting that she should come over to Switzerland, explaining that her husband had less than a 50% chance of survival when he spoke to her. He felt that the odds had lengthened now and that he had something like a 75% chance. The Doctor made it clear that if Len did survive, then he would be paraplegic. He would never walk again and he would need constant care and attention. By all the laws of medicine, he should not have survived the fall; he should not have survived the night on the mountain. He could only marvel at the wonderful level of fitness that had kept him alive and the incredible mental attitude that he had displayed since, to the staff at the hospital.

As she walked from the hospital in the gathering darkness, Brenda weighed the sincere words of the Doctor in her mind. "Paraplegia" ..... "never walk again"..... "lifelong cripple". She knew Len... the Doctor was not talking about her Len. She knew him better than that. He will never give way to these limitations. She knew. Lifting her head to look at the few early stars that were beginning to show their first glimmers to this strange world. "Please God", she thought, "Help him.....please".

Chapter Twelve –

ANGEL OF BERNE

The following day, Brenda met Ruth Brozy. Miss Brozy called each day, as she promised Len she would. She became a constant source of encouragement, both to Len and Brenda. She always had the same 'aura' about her. She radiated hope and was imbued with a dedication that was new to them, even though they were both long-time confirmed Christians. Each visit reinforced their own faith, her words inspiring a glimpse into their future. A future both had doubted a couple of days ago. It was Ruth Brozy who helped them start the ball rolling on their long journey back. They were not sure where she had come from but Len and Brenda were quite sure by Whom she had been sent.

*   *   *   *   *

It was Saturday evening 29th July before Brenda felt sufficiently composed to be able to write a letter to her mother. It was written on notepaper from the hotel – The Pergola, Belpestrasse, Berne.

"Dear Mom,

I expect you are wondering how I am getting on, don't get worrying too much, I am OK The British Embassy are looking after me, but it's a very lonely life. I go to the hospital each day, get there just gone ten. I can come and go as I please, stay till about 2 o'clock and then go and find a place to eat, walk down into Berne and do little bits of shopping and then get back for 4 o'clock and stay till eight at night. Everybody is very kind and a few of the nurses can speak English. It's a marvellous hospital. What can I say about Len? – his neck is broken, his head and face are in a terrible mess, he has had to have stitches in his head, stitches in his leg which they have taken out today. He is just helpless, everything has to be done for him, washed, fed, I give him his food, paper held so he can read. It takes six of them to lift him, eight weights hanging from his head. He may have to have an operation on his neck next week, hope to know more after the weekend. He says he feels very fit in himself and he has got plenty of guts and determination to get through this but it's going to be a very long job – to hear him talk you wouldn't think he had fallen off the Matterhorn, it sounds more like Clent. He is very glad I am here, the days are very long, he just cannot move. Write to him, he would love to hear from you, or the next time Derek phones, go to their house and you can talk to him and me if they ring between 6 and 8. Address for writing is:-

Mr. C.L. York, Insel Hospital, P.Dept. Ward 109, Berne, Switzerland. Don't know when I will be home, probably towards the end of next week, when I have seen the Doctor and they have decided if they are going to do the operation. Must go as I feel very tired and absolutely worn out. Try not to worry too much, look after yourself.

My love to everybody.

> *Lots of love,*
> *Len and Brenda   XXX XXX*

The intensive treatment provided by the superb Insel Hospital Berne began to show signs of laboriously slow progress. Len felt there may be some slight reaction to being prodded in the feet. The lacerations were healing well and he was beginning to look more like his old self. In a few more days the resemblance to a space-man could change, as some of the life-support mechanisms were to be detached. More than a week had passed since his admission. The doctors were warming to Len's sense of humour. "How can you be so happy," they were beginning to ask in a good, clear but rather restricted form of English, "When you cannot move any of your limbs, you are relying on all this apparatus to keep you alive and you are so far from home?"

"Because I can't feel the pain, the apparatus is helping to mend me and God is taking care of me. I have the most supportive visitor I could have in my dear wife and as if that wasn't enough I have met that wonderful Miss Ruth Brozy. Could there be greater reasons for being glad to be alive? God is with me, my friend. He is going to show me the way forward with your help. When can I go home Doctor?"

Strangely, the doctor felt the words fortifying him, because he had harboured doubts for his survival since the moment Len was admitted. Brenda was not surprised by Len's reaction. The words were those he would have used before the accident. What surprised her was that he was capable of such strength at so early a date in his recovery process. She noted that he did not say he was "Going to get better". He said "He is going to show me the way forward". She thought that was significant.

Dr Lanzrein turned from the bed smiling and looked toward Brenda. "Tell me, Mrs York, how has your husband changed since the accident? Is your husband's enthusiasm more, or less than he had before the accident."

Brenda allowed herself a smile, knowing that the Doctor was grappling with an important decision. "He has been the same ever since I met him. One of the most attractive things about Len has always been his enthusiasm for anything with a challenge, and life has always been a challenge to him. When that changes, it could have a big bearing on both of us. In the meantime we soldier on – he hasn't changed one iota!"

"Ah," Doctor Lanzrein raised his right index finger and inclined his head slightly; "We speak the same language! Iota – a Greek word I remember from my days of study". He looked into Brenda's eyes with a new, closer understanding as he spoke the words with a smile. He looked down to Len, "I have been in touch with a hospital in England and we will be able to move you soon. We are intending to discharge you from this hospital on the 7th August, next Monday."

Len was delighted; this was the very first step on the road back. Brenda took the news with a feeling of mixed blessings. She did not want Len to leave this magnificent hospital where they were obviously geared up to be able to treat so precisely, the type of injury her husband had suffered. She knew Len would be happy at the news. Not least because of the removal of the uncertainty of the costs of his treatment. He could only surmise that with no National Health Service comparable to what was available in England, and no technical expertise in being able to sort out the insurance implications of his treatment, he would be better off at home where he knew, roughly, the position. He 'thought' his insurance would pay something.

Brenda's reservations surfaced as she asked quietly. "Do you know which hospital Len will go to in England? The Doctor replied that it had been arranged but he did not know the geography of England too well and if Brenda would go down to his office, the nursing staff would fill in the details for her.

'The Robert Jones and Agnes Hunt Hospital, Oswestry'. Brenda turned over in her mind the name of the hospital she was given by the Swiss staff and inwardly her heart sank. She had never heard of it! What a long way from Halesowen where they lived. How many times a week would she be able to visit her husband over such a distance.... and she not even a driver....well she hadn't passed her test. Why can't he be transferred to the Queen Elizabeth at Edgbaston? Could catch a bus to that hospital.

The Swiss staff had explained, as well as they could, that it was an Orthopaedic Unit and would have special equipment to maintain the treatment they had already started. She walked thoughtfully back to her husband's bedside, beset by further doubts. How can they move him without doing further damage? Will they take him out of his harness? Will she have to push him in a wheelchair? Will anyone else accompany them on the flight? She must put on a show for Len. He must not sense her reservations.

*   *   *   *   *

The Swiss medical team kept their word. Monday 7th August was the day they promised and that was the day it happened. The logistics of moving the supine body, encased from head to thighs, in a plaster cast, was a task of some magnitude. To compound the difficulties, the body talked non-stop. It was a challenge that they set about with the type of vigour of which Len would himself have been proud. Len has been heard to say since, that he thought it was because they were glad to get rid of him! It is likely that this is about as far from the truth as one could get. The medical staff had repeatedly told Brenda that if

Len did not have the level of fitness and the mental approach that he displayed, unfalteringly, whilst he had been in Berne, then they would not have entertained the idea of "letting go of him", as they put it! Each time, they stressed that if those two considerations had not been present, he would not have survived to get as far as their hospital in any case.

At the mention of Oswestry and Shropshire, Len remembered when he was twelve years old. He related the story to Brenda and Ruth Brozy. His school had been evacuated to Oakengates for four months in 1940. It was before Hitler had really got his bombing programme together and before the advent of the 'buzzbombs'. Nevertheless, it was deemed politically expedient to get the youngsters away from areas that attracted the Luftwaffe bombers and children were evacuated from the Smethwick area as often as possible. Smethwick was high on the Fuhrer's list of priorities because of the wealth of industrial talent producing munitions, rolling stock and specialist engineering items that fuelled the war effort of the British troops. So it was that Len's school "Smethwick Junior Technical School" was transported to the relatively safe haven of Shropshire. The final task for the children was set by the head teacher, Mr Tomkinson. He arranged for all the pupils to climb the 'Wrekin', the famous hill that rises from the Shropshire plain. From the direction of Much Wenlock it is easy to see the volcanic formation of the hill, many millions of years old. It looks higher than Clent from that angle and it was the height that caused Len to have reservations about the plans that were being laid for the last day before the children were to return home. The Wrekin is not far from Wenlock Edge, made famous by AE Houseman, and fashioned from a different geological process, which involved the lifting and 'folding' of the limestone rocks. Undoubtedly the four month long stay had been well used to inculcate a certain amount of education into these 'sons of the steelworkers', a number of whom were unaware of the attractions of the rural life.

One of this number was young Charles Leonard York. At thirteen years of age, the task set before him was considered by Len to be uninteresting, and whatsmore he did not feel that at his tender age he was capable of climbing 'Mount' Wrekin anyway. He had enjoyed the time at Oakengates generally, but this was not for him. It was hard work but he managed to persuade his mother into sending a note to the school to excuse him from the trip, "because of his weak chest and asthmatic tendencies".

The man who subsequently climbed the Matterhorn twice!

The story was good, and brilliantly told by Len as usual, but all three of them appreciated the irony, when the words came from the slit they had left in his casing, to facilitate his speech.

Immediately before leaving the hospital at Berne to fly back to the U.K. Len suffered a further bout of despair. His new casing reminded him of the times he went to The Majestic Cinema at Bearwood, on Saturday afternoons, to watch the cowboy films. It would be at much the same time as the school's evacuation to Oakengates. He remembered the number of times he had seen the cowboy hero strapped down before a herd of stampeding buffalo. That is how it felt to be in the casing with no chance of any movement for him! A window cleaner smiled through the large picture panes as he was cleaning them – he waved to Len. Len could not move to respond. He did not feel that he wanted to respond. Why was it him and not the window-cleaner who had had a fall? Window cleaners are always falling from their ladders. They expect to fall. He could not sleep, he was too uncomfortable. He was too ashamed of his thoughts. He apologised mentally to the window-cleaner but it was no good. He would have changed places with anyone at that time. Anyone!

*   *   *   *   *

Brenda arrived at the hospital to be at his side during the return journey and within minutes she was joined by.......the faithful Ruth Brozy. She was full of excited chatter but she did not want to see them go. She was a mixture of elation and sadness. Allowing them privacy as much as that was possible, she maintained a low profile whilst the staff got on with the difficult job of preparing Len for the journey. He needed verbal encouragement as well as physical care. It was to the verbal encouragement that he responded so well. The army of hospital staff walked along endless corridors forming a guard of honour, fussing with lift doors, enjoying jokes at Len's expense, both in English and the Swiss language (or was it German? – neither Len nor Brenda could ever be sure). At last, the brightness of the day burst upon them and Len's eyes were blinded by the bright sun....... and there was no way he could protect himself. Brenda reacted to his anguished shout and walked along holding a newspaper at an angle. This way she was able, at least, to shield his eyes. As they approached the ambulance, a figure stepped in between the vehicle and the stretcher-bed that cradled the helpless form.

It was Ruth Brozy!

She blessed both Len and Brenda; said a short prayer; told him he would recover............... and in a last act of moving faith she sprinkled both of them with the remaining precious drops of holy water, she had brought back from Lourdes. She had saved it especially for them.

The "Angel of Berne" could not know the depth of feeling of Len nor Brenda at that moment. Neither could she know how much the memory of her would haunt them both for the rest of their lives.

Chapter Thirteen –

THE HEARSE

Zurich Airport, 6.30 p.m. Monday 7th August 1972. The plane of the Swiss Air flight took off. By this time, the sunshine that had kept them both company almost continually since Brenda arrived in Berne ten days previously, deserted them at the airport. The smooth take-off had them hurtling through the pall of grey cloud in minutes and above the cloud layer Brenda saw the sun quite low in the west to the left of the plane.

Len saw nothing but the metallic arch of the roof above him. Far below, the setting sun cast a golden light onto the highest of the peaks providing a majestic picture as they rose above the wisps of cloud hugging the valleys between the tops. Brenda provided a running commentary for a short while until she realised what torture it was for Len not to be witnessing this special display. Not to be exercising his mind naming the peaks as they slid slowly from view ten thousand feet below. With every mile that brought them nearer to home, Len sensed an awareness of change. He was emerging slowly from a dream-like existence. He had been seriously injured – oh yes – there was that! What nagged at him was the life of utter luxury that he had experienced in hospital at Berne. His fearful injuries had not bothered him too much in the sense that pain was spasmodic and rare, partly because his central nervous system was failing to warn him. Neither he nor Brenda had been waited on in any shape or form, at any time in their lives, apart from the unselfish ministrations of their respective moms when they were living at home. They did not live in the strata of society that expected and received constant attention. Waiters stung into action on a whim, or cleaning staff to save them the task of emptying the bin, were never part of their lifestyle. Living on a council housing estate, as they did in the formative years, or later in their own semi-detached comfortable property in Halesowen had taken much of their earnings. But never, in any aspect of their lives previously, had they been subjected to the level of creature comforts, showered on them from the hospital. It was a level of support and attention that had kept him alive and that was the level of attention that all hospital patients received as normal in Switzerland it seemed. No Health Service like ours, so the staff had to put on a good show to survive – and how they did! He was an embound chrysalis slowly emerging from all this. How slowly? How completely?............ One thing was sure, his lips moved into a tight curve as the humour of the situation gripped him. "You won't emerge as a beautiful butterfly" he told himself.

"What was that you mumbled about a butterfly?" asked Brenda. He was shocked that he must have spoken the words out loud but obviously sufficiently slurred, and suitably baffled by the noise of the aircraft, to just elude Brenda's grasp.

"You're not starting to ramble are you?"

"No. I just feel a bit tired. It has been a big day after all. I think I'll try to get some sleep before we have the next upheaval at Manchester...... Brenda!"

"Yes Len?"

He was still restricted to expressions emanating only from his eyes. They flicked to her direction and he held her gaze. "I shall never be out of your debt!" He managed to move his fingers almost imperceptibly, but Brenda leaned forward, took the fingers between both hands, looked firmly into his eyes with a mixture of penetrating tenderness and admiration. "Don't be so daft!" she chided. "You would do the same for me". Their eyes kissed, glazed over and Len closed his, partly so that she would not see the emotion, partly to savour the special moment, partly to hide his fear and mostly so that he could drift into sleep for the rest of the journey.

*   *   *   *   *

Brenda didn't sleep. Her inner feelings mirrored so much of what Len was thinking. She could not for the life of her see what was to happen in the next few years, in the next few weeks, in the next few hours. Apprehensive, even that the door to their special flight cubicle might open and produce more problems for them. "Hadn't they got enough on their plate? What was to happen at Manchester? How would they get him off the plane? Would there be enough people to help her? When would Len be able to eat? To hell with eating – she couldn't touch a thing tonight. God let us get over this! "she thought.

It was still only about 9 o'clock when Brenda stepped out of the plane. The hour difference from continental time had worked to their advantage – except that it extended a difficult day by the same period and tiredness was now becoming a serious factor for both of them. The Manchester skies had darkened to a deep dusk. There was no sign of an ambulance.

Two men in peaked caps and heavy coats boarded the plane and introduced themselves. It was the official Government reception committee. "We are from Customs and Excise – Have you anything to declare?" They hesitated for a moment, and for once in his life Len was unable to take advantage of the situation with some apt comment. He was so appalled that they had nothing better to do! He was speechless! They looked at Brenda; they looked back at Len. The silence must have told them more than either of them would have communicated if they could have spoken!

The men shuffled away muttering something about "being sorry."

"Why are they sorry?" Len asked Brenda. "Cos they haven't found anything? Do they know where to start looking? Perhaps they've gone back to find some tools to get into this plaster cast?"

*   *   *   *   *

The airport staff met the plane and began the painstaking job of lifting their charge from the aircraft without causing any more damage than was absolutely necessary. They had been well warned and equally well trained for the moment. The manoeuvre was completed with surprising speed and dexterity and they waited for the ambulance for a few minutes.

While they waited, a group of girl guides were disembarking to the tarmac. Their leader saw the wheeled stretcher waiting in the warmth of the darkening night and without breaking her step she walked across the level surface to Len's side. She peered into the slits in the casing to make sure there really was someone inside, rested her hand on the hard shell that represented the head and said "God Bless You – whoever you are!" She turned on her heel, returned to her group of chattering youngsters and Len was stung to the heart by the youthful freshness of the crowd making their way to the terminal. How often he and Brenda had been in the same situation, shepherding a group of youngsters – male and female – to the most remote parts – and always how they had enjoyed those times.

He was bought quickly to his senses when the ambulance arrived. Neither of them recognised it at first. Instead of the white, bulbous, large van-like vehicle that was familiar to them, the hospital had sent their own low, long wheelbase, stout black Leyland vehicle. It had a sliding mechanism which was heaved out from the back and gently coaxed into position within two yards of the stretcher. Brenda was horrified. It seemed her deep reservations about returning home had been realised before the first hurdle.

It was a .... hearse?

*　　*　　*　　*　　*

Their arrival at the Robert Jones and Agnes Hunt Orthopaedic Hospital, in the darkness, in the "hearse", was a cheerless affair. The vehicle turned right into the main entrance, past a row of shed buildings. Brenda thanked God silently that Len could not see the place. It looked like a series of Nissen huts in the blackness. At best it would be described as "resembling a disused army barracks." The physical contrast with the "palace" that they had left earlier in the day at Berne could not have been more marked. The driver reversed the vehicle expertly into the entrance to one of the huts.

First appearances were sombre indeed. Len was being pushed by the vehicle driver, assisted by hospital porters, to his new home. Where else could it be in a Shropshire Hospital but "Wrekin" ward. The name of the hill he refused to climb was beginning to haunt him, more than thirty years later.

Both Brenda and Len were to find qualities in the hospital they could not possibly have anticipated! Wrekin ward in particular!
In the anti-room, by prior arrangement, Brenda's brother-in-law Derek was waiting to transport Brenda back to the Midlands for her first night at home in almost two weeks.......... facing how long a period of grass-widowhood?

She was to find qualities within her that she could not possibly have anticipated!

*   *   *   *   *

A surprise for Len was the sight of David, his younger brother, accompanied by their brother-in-law, Jack. The pair were allowed into the anti-room to talk with Len for a short time, before the doors were closed on Charles Leonard York for his first night in hospital in England. Despite all the efforts of the staff to accept and make him feel comfortable, Len was certain that the immediate future would not be anything but a long, hard uphill struggle. Not the type of climb he was used to.

He was to find he had qualities within him that he could not possibly have anticipated!

Chapter Fourteen –

INSPIRATION

After two and a half days in The Robert Jones and Agnes Hunt hospital at Oswestry, the operation was performed to remove the 'Minerva' from the patient. Len had recovered from the first view of the "hearse". He realised quite soon, after the initial reaction, that it was the best type of vehicle in which he could have been transported. Specially adapted to carry paraplegics and seriously disabled bodies, it was part of the essential trappings of a hospital that was striving to cope with the demands of the 1970s whilst working out of buildings that resembled Nissen huts from the back end of the 1940s.

The initial reservations he had were brought sharply into focus when he saw the youthful nurse bearing down on him with a tool that would have done credit to the name of any hand-held power drill. A saw-blade was attached to the business end. The nurse brandishing the weapon, leaned toward him and told him with a theatrical wave and an air of confidentiality, "I haven't done this before!" A moment of sheer panic overtook the patient before his logic told him that what she intended to convey was that she was quite used to the job of removing plaster casts but she had not had to remove a full 'Minerva' before.

Didn't she?

Len was immediately conscious of the vulnerability of his neck when the cast was removed. He was a rag-doll. He didn't have sufficient strength to stop his head rolling to one side on the pillow. It had been supported since his admission to the Insel Hospital Berne until a few minutes before and he could not wait for the operation to re-set the head with spring-loaded callipers. More holes had to be drilled into the skull to accommodate the harness clips. Each step was forecast by the staff, to "keep him in the picture" as they said. It didn't help. At Berne, Len had been in a coma when the initial "setting" of the neck was performed. He was in traction when he woke up at Berne but he was wide-awake at Oswestry and was warned of every detail. He still felt no pain because there was still an absence of feeling.

"How brave you are Len!" These were the words written to him by so many of his friends and relatives whilst he was in Oswestry and each day his postbag increased. He was very well blessed with friends and even more blessed with a closely-knit and supportive family.

"How brave you are Len!" These were the words so often spoken at the side of his bed by the succession of visitors.

"Not so!" responded Len. "Bravery is not when you are lying here. It's Hobson's choice to be lying here making the most of a bad job. If you want to talk to me about bravery, talk to me about the heroics that went on in the war – on both sides. Talk to me about someone like George Cloughley who found himself on a strange mountain, in a strange country, at eight o'clock at night. At twelve thousand feet. He had a colleague on the end of a rope. Or he thought he had. He had to go and climb down a precipitous face to find him, make sure he was alive. Tie him as a dead weight to the face of the rock and then descend. On his own! To a point where he could get help. At 10 o'clock at night. And do it successfully. Now that's bravery!".

*   *   *   *   *

The two Dons – Don Haskins, chauffeured by Don Saunders, visited the hospital at Oswestry about two weeks into Len's stay. In a few weeks time they would be paying their annual pilgrimage to the Highlands and, as he would not accompany them this year, they felt a spot of advice from "Yorkie" would not go amiss. Not being quite sure of their reception (they thought they knew how badly injured he was) they were a little muted on their journey through the slow, evening, Shrewsbury Bye-pass, traffic.

Don Haskins was thinking over the way in which he had been introduced to Len. Through his interest in running, he had joined the Halesowen Athletic Club at Manor Way. He was the "new boy" although mature enough to have seen the last of thirty-five summers. He remembered getting changed in the dressing rooms after a particularly heavy training session just after he had joined the club. It was always the same group of athletes who dominated the shower room after the workout and it was always the same tenor voice that seemed to cut through the steam above the shouts of all the others. They were usually swopping stories about who had cut up the other on the track, or how well they had run at the weekend, or where they were going next weekend. It was always Yorkie who had them all in rapt attention. It was usually Yorkie who was bearing the brunt of the slanderous taunts they threw about. It was always Yorkie who came out and sat talking to Don before they made their individual way home. Unknown to each other at that time, they had both suffered as children with asthmatic tendencies. It was interesting that, from different starting points, each had gravitated towards the open air as adults, to catch up on what they felt they had missed in earlier years. It was Len who first asked Don if he had done any fell walking. "If you have any ambitions that way, why don't you come and join us when we go to Scotland in September?" invited Len.

Don did, and if he thought he was going on a holiday, he was soon to find out that this was anything but the relaxation most people seek when they go to Scotland for a week. He was glad he had talked Don Saunders into leaving his wife and family for a few days to join them, otherwise he could have been left back at the youth hostel each day when the onslaught started. Not content with tackling some of the real "testers" in the Highlands, the group found it more of a challenge to go up "the hard way" rather than the tourist tracks. They would set off at eight o'clock in the morning, whatever the weather. They had expected an early start. What had surprised the two Dons was that this all took place after they had originally bounded out of bed at six a.m. to indulge themselves in a five-mile run before breakfast. Just to get in the mood for the day's climbs! The Dons had found this all rather bewildering at first and Len would often stay behind with them on the walks. They would allow the bulk of the party to "blooter off" as they put it. The aim was to establish who could get to the top quickest and arguably by the most difficult route!

Don remembered Len being more thoughtful. He would point out the beauties of the landscape and encourage the younger men to take in the freshness of the air and appreciate the smells, the feel and the sounds. He particularly loved the fauna of the area. Don recalled Len's fascination one day with a herd of Lap-deer. They showed none of the nervous tendencies of the native strain. Len was able to get close enough to feed these huge beasts from his hand, whereas the Scottish deer tended to depart the scene at dizzying pace when the human forms were still two miles away.

Don Haskins was temporarily obliged to forget those thoughts as Don Saunders expertly guided his car to the only available spot in the car park at the hospital. They were ushered into the starkly quiet atmosphere of the ward where all the beds were occupied by very poorly patients. They were glad the nurse offered to take them to the bedside, as they would undoubtedly not have recognised their friend. They tried to steel themselves for the occasion and however light-hearted they tried to be they were both desperately short of the right words when they approached the prone figure on the bed. The contraptions fixed into his head and seemingly into his body all along his side to his feet, restrained him from any movement.

"Len?" Don Haskins' slightly husky voice was tight and he was more restricted than usual in his delivery. His one-word statement was more of a question, as if he had been told it was he, but he didn't believe it. To his shame, he felt that he wanted to turn round and leave the ward in the one-second silence that greeted him, so inadequate did he feel. "Come on Don H, get yourself a chair and make yourself comfortable. Tell Don S to get himself settled, I know he'll be with you. Yo'm like a pair o' twins, yo two" said Len, lapsing into an untypically hard Black Country idiom. "I've got some questions for you to answer." It *was* Yorkie, this strip of wind that hardly showed any form at all under the bedclothes. The talking head that could not move apart from it's eyes. That couldn't eat apart from sucking liquids through a straw. That all-action, all talking, all singing, all dancing larger than life mountain climber and marathon distance runner. He could blink his eyelids and he could talk. After that there was no movement from start to finish of the interview. They had intended to stay for a couple of hours but sensed that it was too much for Len. After half an hour of tremendously hard work for all three of them they had answered a few questions, given Len a few facts, left with him the useless grapes for his visitors to consume and walked out of the hospital in silence.

It took until they were settled in the car again for either of them to speak. Don S did not turn the ignition key. They just sat and looked at each other. They were still hearing the words of the physio who had come to administer to Len. They had used that as the reason for their departure and the physio told them that he was trying hard to get Len NOT to exercise his limbs. The man had told them "Len is so keen to get moving and walking again that he will not stop trying to move himself about; whilst the whole idea of his recovery at present is to keep him still. He keeps trying to move his parts" he said. "No-one can fault this man's enthusiasm for life," he continued, "He can't wait to get on the move again and run you blokes off your feet! He has to learn to pace himself – all over again!"

"You can't beat this bloke, can you Don!" said Haskins to Saunders, at last breaking the silence and permitting himself a wry smile. "It reminds me when we were in Scotland last year – you remember – when we went to Skye, the three of us. You know he always knows everybody. He kept saying he wanted to see Ronald MacDonald, and you made some facetious comment about his hamburgers. Len was quite put out at your ignorance, but he did his best to put us right, didn't he! 'I thought everyone knew him,' Len had said. 'He is the boatman, he delivers the groceries, the papers, fetches you stamps, carries messages, gets the Doctor if you're ill.... he's a brilliant fellow – everybody knows him!' He was so determined to see him and introduce us to him, but you thought he was romancing" said Haskins.

"Yes he did get on my nerves about him," said Saunders, "why does he always seem to know everybody?"

His eyes creased into a knowing smile as Haskins kept the story going by reminding him. "Then we went to Glen Brittle that night when it poured with rain. It was like midnight at about half-past seven in the evening. Jet-black! Do you remember?"

Of course Saunders remembered........ they were both already chuckling.

"The rain was like stair-rods." went on Haskins. "I have never seen rain like it! Before nor since! The road was flooded – about three inches deep! It had been raining all day."

"Then we came to that gated road in Glen Brittle, the one with the slate gate-post next to it." Saunders had now taken up the tale. "It was so dark at this point that we started to withdraw from the privilege of being the one to open the gate. As we came to a stop, the slate gate-post moved, stuck out an arm, and opened the gate!"

"What an effect it had on Yorkie!" interrupted Haskins, his voice going up an octave. "He was jumping about in the front seat like something demented. I thought he had seen a Ghost!"

They both laughed uproariously at this point, at the vision of the precious moment they had shared.

"I thought he'd gone yampy!" said Saunders with a malicious smile. "Then he told us the gatepost was Ronald MacDonald!

They collapsed into convulsions and anyone in the car park at the time who witnessed their antics would have wondered if he were at the Orthopaedic or Mental Hospital.

It was some minutes before they regained their composure sufficiently to start the car. Saunders turned the key, looked at Haskins and enquired seriously "Shall we ever have moments like that with him again, I wonder?" He knocked the car into reverse, manoeuvred, slid the gear into the forward mode and they were on their way to their comfortable homes.

"He is as much an inspiration now as he ever was!" said Haskins, "What a fighter!"

There was no time for boredom on the way home. They swopped stories about Len for the duration of the hour and a half journey, and they didn't stop laughing.

*   *   *   *   *

It was about six weeks into his stay at Oswestry and his progress, he thought, had been little better than "zero". It was September 21st 1972 to be exact. The 21st of September was the date that he would have been paid his monthly salary. He always arranged to go to Scotland for a week climbing with friends during the week of the 21st, to be sure he would have enough money in his pocket to pay for the extras that invariably cropped up. It was a particularly warm day for early autumn, his favourite time of the year. Brenda would come and visit him that night, he knew, but that was some hours away and his imagination drifted into a reverie, as he lay, under the glass canopy of the veranda roof. The veranda was open-sided and the staff were very quick to "give the patients some air" if the weather was good. The hospital had been a "TB" isolation hospital in it's day – probably in the forties and fifties – hence the rare facility for the luxury of "open-air" treatment.

The silence was broken only by the hum of insects and the occasional heavier droning of bees visiting the mature beds of roses that ran the length of the side wards. He raised one eyelid sufficiently to make sure that his recently acquired friend, Ted Thompson, was taking the air. He was there – he lay on his bed about twenty yards away, his wife watching for any wasp that may feel it had a future in landing on Ted. He had suffered a crippling injury too, and he would not have known if a wasp had stung him, such was his separation from his nervous system. Ted's wife wafted the nectar collectors away before they could do any damage. "What a prospect," thought Len, he knew just how serious were Ted's injuries and sympathised with the man's wife. He thought how lucky he was that there were some prospects for himself, something to aim for.

As his mind drifted back to enjoy the moment, he caught sight of John Lawrence, the ward orderly, busily moving about the campus. John was about 6 feet 4 inches tall and a "big" man in every sense. He had a big heart set in that big frame of his. He loved the job he was doing. Nothing was too much trouble for him. Len would summon him in the depths of night, when other patients were deep in sleep. John would, on his own, turn Len over, tuck him in again, make sure he was comfortable and fetch anything legal that Len wanted. After a night "dancing attendance" on those needing it, he had to go home to his wife and family at the most unearthly hour. "What a tough job," thought Len, but how lucky was John to be in a job that he obviously loved so much. How lucky the hospital to have this "round peg in the round hole". How lucky was Len to be on the receiving end of the attention and care that this man lavished on him and the other patients. Len always had the greatest respect for the work done by the paramedics and the ancillaries and often wondered what it was that brought them into the caring profession. It seemed to him that their rewards never quite matched up to the amount of work and effort they put into everything they did. He could see the rewards presented when a patient showed a remarkable improvement or full recovery but what when a patient didn't improve? It made no difference to the amount of effort the orderly put in. Len was right to count his blessings – it was a philosophy that would serve him well.

He settled back again, beguiled by the subtle ambience. A ballet of nature was being performed around him. The soft balm of a breeze on his face, occasionally wafting the heavy perfume of hybrid tea into his nostrils. He had admired the display of roses since the first day he had been allowed out into the veranda. "Best things you've got in any of the beds here," he had remarked to the nursing staff. He couldn't see the blooms from where he was lying, but he pictured them in his mind's eye. He dozed. The enigma was starting again. The picture gently fused with mountains and focused the reverie to Scotland again. It was as if he was looking through his camera lens. There would be the two Dons – Haskins and Saunders, Alan Plant, and perhaps Bob Duncan and John Wagstaff. At that time of day, early afternoon, they would have done the bulk of the "work" for the day. Would they have climbed to the top of "The Ben" by the back route and be well on the way down to Fort William for haggis and chips and the subsequent entertainment that could provide? He chuckled inwardly. Would they have motored on to Torridon by now? Could they have had a day on Ben Eighe or walked down the corrie to Kinlockewe. Some of the oldest mountains known to man. On a day like this if they take their time coming down to the hostel they will see one of the finest sunsets in the world. Something special happens when half of the sun slips into the sea. The red light skims across the dappled water and the effect is enhanced when the light reaches the Torridon sandstone. The great fireball lends red on red to a landscape that was an artist's delight before the unreal effect added by this natural flood of stage lighting.

Len had led the group last year. They had been so impressed by the sunset they were bubbling like a bunch of enthusiastic schoolboys when the warden at the hostel got involved in the discussion. He regaled them for a half an hour about the superb sights he had seen there over the years, before ending with "But ye have ta see em, don't ye!" – and with a practised flourish of his dish cloth he turned back to the scouring of the table tops. Implicit it was in his last remark that anyone who hasn't been to that corner of the world has missed a jewel.

"A jewel – yes! That was how we had described it ourselves," remembered Len, just a might wistfully. "The biggest jewel we had ever seen" he repeated to himself mistily. He dwelt on the thoughts, turned them over again inwardly. He questioned his place with those heroes of his in the future. When will he be able to share the esoteric pleasures at the sights and the sounds, cope with vagaries of wind and weather, thrill to a view from the summit, and find again that inner satisfaction from a challenging climb? How long would it be? Would he ever manage it again? There was feeling in his head and face and he felt a chemical reaction taking place in his cheeks. His bottom lip moved, the stiff upper lip crinkled. There was no time to check whether anyone was watching. He could not get beneath the sheet to hide the emotions that enveloped the few feeling parts of him.

He sobbed!

He should have been leading the group again this year – now! Not for the first time in his adult life the 'toughie' who ran marathons, the fearless conqueror of the Matterhorn – twice – felt the salt tears flooding down his face and into his mouth as he convulsed into a fathomless black pit of wretched despair.

He was ravaged. He couldn't run away from it. Money could not buy him freedom from it.

It was his lowest point.

He was alive – yet he was dead.

Chapter Fifteen –

THE CHAIR

Len had been at Oswestry for three months. The November mornings had seen off much of the beauty of the gardens surrounding the hospital. There were dustings of white frost lingering on the lawns until early afternoon in the shaded areas.

A couple of weeks earlier the staff had been able to remove the calipers from Len's head, and the harness was removed. Before he had time to savour the wonderful feeling of release, the nurses were bending him in the middle to create a new "L" shaped Len. "L for Len is it then?" he was caught, panting out his humour. "All I can say is thank God I am not named Ulysees."

The staff were beginning to love him. His indomitable will, his humour, his encouragement of the rest of the patients and his own glimmerings of a recovery (of sorts) were starting to spark his old personality. He was finding it possible to relax, just a touch, in his mind whilst he still was trying to cope with fearsome physical odds. The "L" shaped Len was permitted to remain "L" shaped for one hour only. An hour during which he was terrified to turn his head. He had become used to the full support that the callipers and harness had provided for several months and he felt that if he allowed the rag-doll neck to drop, his head would sever completely, the weight of his head having no muscle to support it. The nursing staff were unmerciful in their insistence that he turn his neck and gradually work up the power on the muscles. Even loquacious Len could not find a word to describe his abject horror at the prospect.

The nurses became his sergeant-majors. They had for long enough cocooned and treated him with too much respect. There was at first, they thought, a chance that he would not be with them for long. Then, against the odds he lasted days, then weeks, then months.

He confounded all doctors with his will to survive and he was now showing signs that he could improve his condition with his unique level of basic fitness. Even with all the plusses he had working for him, it would not be possible to improve his mobility on his own. The staff were aware of this and Brenda, in particular, was quick to acknowledge it. So the new breed of gently bullying females emerged.

At the three-month milestone since his arrival at Oswestry, his wheelchair arrived.

He hated the whole idea of it!

The prospect of being wheeled about, or wheeling himself about, he did not buy. He was going to walk! He wasn't going to be an invalid, no thanks. But he would just "give it a try".

They got him into it. He was hopeless! His arms hadn't an ounce of strength in them! He didn't have enough to provide the motive power needed just to get him along the corridor.

In his frustration, he sat in the corridor outside Wrekin Ward pulling and pushing the gadgets, softly cursing under his breath; he damned well *would* get the wheels turning if it was the last thing he did. His concentration was so focused he didn't notice the appearance of a figure standing a few feet away. The man watched for a few seconds, smiling at Len's antics.

"You can do better than that Yorkie." he said.

"I damn well can't" said Len, thinking it was one of the hospital orderlies. But hospital orderlies didn't call him 'Yorkie' – it was 'Len' or 'Mr York'. Len looked up to see a smiling John Wagstaffe. A welcome visitor at any time, Len held out his right hand toward him and said. "John, my old friend – what providence – you've been sent to get me out of this mess – good on ya!" Then Len noticed something not quite right about him. John hadn't walked spontaneously towards him but moved with a pronounced 'hobble'. He had one of his legs in plaster. He had a broken leg! "Are you a patient or a visitor?" asked Len. "Have you come to push my wheelchair, or are you expecting me to push you?"

John answered with his actions. He knew he had the physical advantage over Len, just as surely as he knew he never had, and never would have, the verbal advantage. He hobbled to the wheelchair, took it by the handles, and despite his temporary encumbrance, was able to push Len around what seemed miles of hospital corridors. Before he left for home, he wheeled Len outside and faced him in a westerly direction. This was so that he faced the Welsh Mountains where they had spent so many happy hours together in the past. Len thought that his first day in the wheelchair had been quite fun, after all. Perhaps he could accept it as a temporary expedient, on the way to full recovery!

*   *   *   *   *

The orderlies got Len to the gym. They laid him on the floor. They told him to roll over from his back to his stomach and then back again. They were delighted when he did it.

It took him one and a half days!

Len was almost in a state of despair again at his inability to perform the most mundane of exercises. He was impatient. He always did have the tendency to be impatient. No doubt this is why he achieved so much in his life. However, he was to find that Sergeant Majors also have ways of achieving results. After a number of days lying on the floor with a dumb-bell across his throat he was able to move it up and down reasonably well and the recovery process kick-started again.

Len, despite his tendency to impatience, was beginning to appreciate the staff and the methods employed at the Robert Jones and Agnes Hunt Hospital. He accepted that it was "different" from the luxurious "Hotel" that had provided his bed in Switzerland but it had a charm of its own. It was rich with dedicated staff. It specialised in the problems of the paraplegic. How wrong both he and Brenda had been to doubt the wisdom of being repatriated to Oswestry. It had become his lifeline!

*   *   *   *   *

It took days to train him into sitting in the chair comfortably, but as the strength in his arms improved, Len found it easier. He still didn't like the wheelchair. "The longer you stay in the wheelchair, the longer you will stay in a wheelchair" was Len's philosophy. In a surprisingly short time, by sitting between the "walls" of a walking frame and heaving himself up, he was able to get almost to a standing position. He was encouraged by the gym staff to keep at the exercises until, supported by splints for his legs, he was able to stand in the frame.

He did this several times a day until he could stand for a full hour – still in splints. It would have been easier to pack up his troubles in one of the sergeant major's kit bags, throw in the towel and go back to bed for the rest of his life. It would mean that life wouldn't last too long – not life, as Len wanted to live it.

He was happier learning to live all over again.

He was a baby, with adult problems. He had to learn to fall and throw away his elbow crutches as he got nearer to the floor, to take the weight on his strengthening hands and arms. Then he found he could "walk" a few yards, purely by the strength in his arms, on the elbow crutches. Then he was allowed to go outside into the fresh air for a short "stand". One day he "walked", with the weight entirely on his hands and arms, on the crutches. In this way he was able to manage the whole length of the corridor at the hospital – still with the help of splints on those bloody legs of his which were so useless.

Len knew that if he applied himself, the body would take it. From a bad start in life, he had learned to live with that body, learned to trust its strengths, nurtured it to a level of fitness that most people could not even conceive. Now he was starting again. Now he must do it without splints. His right leg did not want to bend and his foot had "dropped" on the end of his leg bones. He wasn't to know that his legs would never walk for him. He would not have believed anyone who told him so at this stage of his regeneration. He didn't even want to know about anything negative. That was no way to beat a problem!

He found a champion in the form of the Head of the Department of Occupational Therapy at the hospital. A lady by the name of Jill Arnott. Her patience and encouragement were an inspiration to Len and he found it difficult to believe that the kindness she showed to him was repeated with the same dedication to all the other patients she had to deal with. Not for one day, not for one week, not for one year but for all the working life of this wonderful person.

The first idea that she presented to Len was for him to get involved with the basket making and furniture production. This met with little enthusiasm from her patient. He told her that he had a job to get back to. He was Chief Design Draughtsman at an important firm in the Black Country and he wanted to concentrate on improving the fine skills for his stiff fingers. He needed to get back to the subtleties of pen wielding and would she concentrate on that please? He didn't particularly want to get involved in "making things" and could she devise some way of getting the digits working again.

Forever the optimist!

She started by drawing a line on a piece of card, handed him a pair of scissors and said, "OK – Just show me how well you can cut along that line!" The stiff and mangled fingers managed to hold the paper in the left hand. The sheer effort of using the right hand to squeeze together the blades caused beads of perspiration to form on his brow. It was incongruous that anyone should think those misshapen wooden pegs on the extremity of the arms would work like normal fingers but they did, sufficiently for him to prove yet another point. He could do things sufficiently well, however slowly, to make it worthwhile for her to support him and find new challenges for him. He certainly rose to the challenge! The next job that was presented to him was to polish up iron rods that were to be used to modify a wheelchair in order to provide armrests for another patient. This was done by using progressively fine grades of emery papers. Dexterity was returning and the fingers, although they would always be misshapen and stiff, they were deceptively manipulative. After a short period of rehabilitation he was introduced to the fretsaw – one that required a co-ordination between a treadle arrangement to provide the motive power, and finger work to keep the cutting blade on course. Jill Arnott would tie Len's feet onto the pedals but she couldn't help with the lack of comfort on the saddle. He could not feel the seat at all because of the lack of feeling in the seat area and was always afraid that he was about to slide off it at any moment.

Those days were shared with George Brown, a man who was a railway maintenance worker. He had broken his back, when a signal post on which he was working collapsed because it had rotted through at ground level. He was working on the signal arm at the time and as the post fell to the ground he tried to jump clear. The post caught him and caused him a serious spinal injury. He was a man of great physical strength and the two found comfort in shared experiences and complementary sense of humour. Both Len and George were determined to recover as much of their fitness as possible and always they were the last pair to leave the gym, usually being chased out by Mrs Springall who had responsibility for the gymnasium and it's equipment. She was a lady of formidable reputation and discipline and how she needed to be! These two characters would have stayed in the gym all night if she had allowed them to get away with it. It was particularly difficult to get them out of the warmth of the building and into the dark night air in their wheelchairs, when they had to negotiate frost and ice on the long driveway from the gym to the main block. They became proficient at negotiating the slippery surface outside the building, but Mrs Springall was far too quick for them when they attempted to charge around the gym in their wheelchairs to avoid having to leave. Neither patient was strong enough in the arms yet to outrun being unceremoniously "dumped" outside the main exit in the cold air! But it was fun trying!

*   *   *   *   *

By February 1973 Len was much more able to help himself and he learned that his idol Chris Bonington was giving a talk at the Town Hall, Birmingham. The talk was to cover the expedition to Everest – South-West Face which he and his team undertook in November 1972. Len sought the permission of his surgeon to attend and he agreed – provided that Len returned to hospital before 12 noon on the day following the talk. Len was heard to say, "You don't like losing good patients do you?" His surgeon responded, "If you don't show a bit of respect around here I shall take your sticks off you and you will go no-where!" The line was delivered with such a knowing look from the friendly eye of the medical man that Len considered this signified another landmark in his recovery.

Friends liaised with the town hall management who were ultra co-operative in providing the tickets. They also agreed to make arrangements to receive a wheelchair climber and even provided a car-parking space alongside the building. Reg Whitworth, a friend of many years offered to do the 130-mile round trip to Oswestry (twice) to provide transportation. Reg had always been an inspiration to Len since the day when Len decided to join the choir at St Hilda's. The tender recruit saw Reg as a mentor. To Len he was so experienced, this "man" who was all of two years older than he and such a good leader. Brenda Reg and Len were seated in time for the 7.30 start. It was a tonic for Len to be seated in a Hall as capacious and crowded as this and the atmosphere had him leaning forward in his chair even before the lights dimmed to herald the appearance of his hero. He remembered having similar feelings of unbridled anticipation, in the same hall, twenty-five years earlier, when waiting for the Ted Heath Band to take the stage with Lita Rosa, Dickie Valentine and Dennis Lotis. A different motivation that time but he could feel in the atmosphere of the evening that the occasion about to commence would be just as fresh in another twenty-five years time.

The slide show of the Himalayas was breathtaking at times and the commentary was well up to the team's normal excellent standard. Consummate professionals to a man! They explained how they had come to the decision to abort that particular climb of the Southwest Face at a height of 27,300 feet.

It wasn't the first time that Len had been in the company of Chris Bonington. He had spoken to him at a meeting of the British Mountaineering Club in North Wales. The great man came down to see Len after the Birmingham talk and was extremely concerned to see him in a wheelchair. Len was able to tell him at length of the accident on the Matterhorn seven months earlier and Chris summoned his team of the evening to come down to talk to Len and Brenda and sign their programmes for the evening. They still have the programmes in their treasury of a scrap book (which runs to three volumes). They show the following inscriptions:

"All the best and a quick recovery"
Signed. Christian Bonington
Signed. Kelvin Kent

Signed. Dougal Haston
> Who was successful in climbing the same south-west face
> on 24th September 1975 and was tragically killed in a
> ski-ing accident in Switzerland January 1976.

Signed. Mike Burke
> Died on Everest 26th September 1975. Cameraman to
> the expedition. Last seen within 300 feet of the top, still
> moving upwards in deteriorating conditions.

Chapter Sixteen –

OBSESSION

November saw the end of "L" shaped Len and by early Spring 1973 he had straightened to a point where he stood, with the aid of his elbow crutches, only slightly hunched at the shoulders. He had passed through the barrier of negotiating stairs and steps. He was able to sit at the bottom of the hospital steps, in the wheelchair, get up onto his sticks and negotiate a way up twelve steps. His legs would still not work other than to provide a "prop" whilst the bulk of the weight and movement were provided by a forward momentum that he was able to generate from the strength of his arms.

He needed a very special strength in his arms. His pedigree for this could not have been more apt. Much of his physical strength had been inherited from his granddad. In turn granddad inherited his arm strength from his father (Len's Great Grandfather). Both had been miners in the late nineteenth and early twentieth century, working in mines in the West Bromwich and Smethwick border areas. Great Granddad had made a particularly successful job of it by retiring as Manager of the "Jubilee" pit at Wasson Pool. John Drew was the grandfather of Len's mother. As a very young boy, Len was taken by his mother to visit his Great Granddad. It was a rare privilege in 1929. Few youngsters were fortunate enough to remember seeing anyone older than their grandparents.

Len's mother, Abigale, left the Number '200' Midland Red Bus at it's terminus in Stoney Lane, near to the old "Blue Gates" Hotel on Smethwick High St, and installed a sleepy Len in his pushchair. She took care to tuck him into the pushchair with the crocheted blanket to protect his suspect chest and walked the mile and a half to her own mother's house at Carlton Road on the side of the main railway line.

Although number "17" Carlton Road, it was the first house on the left from the Halfords Lane end. It seems that plans were tabled to build other properties along the bank of the railway to start Carlton Road at number one and link up with number 17, but the properties were never built. The "Opening", as the road was referred to just at that point, alongside the "Olde House at Home" pub, had not been adopted by the council. It always presented a rutted track of an approach to the house in which Len's granddad and grandma lived. A house that always harboured magical thoughts and reminiscences for Len in later years. He had spent nights with brothers, cousins, and uncles, sleeping head to tail. "Sardines" in a bed which was completely inadequate for the number of bodies that had usually become stranded after a family outing to the grandparents home. Usually, it happened following a family game of cards during which the children had been allowed to stay up too late to catch the last bus home. The children would be sufficiently tired to be quite indifferent to their comfort and would sleep soundly until morning. If the weather was fine the morning would give an opportunity to engage in another of their favourite occupations. They would "spot the trains" from the top of the bank that formed the long back garden to the house.

The bank looked enormously steep to Len in his childhood. The engines were in full steam when they passed Granddad's house and were invariably travelling fast. They always seemed to be on time but it was a practised art to get the right number and name as the engine thundered past. The difficulty was chiefly caused by the highly intoxicated state of excitement of the would-be "spotters".

Abigale found the progress over the "steps" difficult to negotiate with Len in the pushchair. The "steps", built of "Staffordshire Blue" brick, avoided the long walk round the High Street junction with Rolfe Street. They were steep and demanding even to a fit person. When a young mom had to negotiate the hazard with a pushchair and no help, it was a daunting task. Had Len been awake he would have demanded to stop, young though he was. He would let his mom know that he wanted to be lifted up to watch the train pass through the tunnel below the bridge which was formed by the walkway. The winkle seller's barrow was parked in the cul-de-sac fashioned by the position of the "steps", outside the "George" Public House. This presented another fascination for the young child ... especially if the winkle man's horse was in the area! Once quietly past these two possible hold-ups, the walk up Brasshouse Lane to Carlton Road would present only the problem of the steep hill up to the "Waggon and Horses" pub.

The cup of tea that her mother had prepared was nectar to Abigale after the long haul. The temperature was improving and the prospect was for a warm day by noon on a clear blue summer day. Abigale knew that ahead lay a further walk of at least four miles down the twisting lanes to Wasson Fields. As it was such a nice day her mother, also Abigale, decided to walk with them. She had used the last of her eggs and if luck was with her, there would be a few duck eggs at the cottage by the pool. Even though the weather was fine the two women fussed around the pushchair, tucking Len in with another blanket. It was a good walk and if a cool wind blew up it could play havoc with his chest. They were worried that this first born son of Charles and Abigale was prone to colds and had suffered a series of them during the winter. The colds kept recurring, well into the spring of 1931. The residual cough had an asthmatic sound to it and they were taking no chances. One did not take chances on the health of the young when the infant mortality rate was so high. Len's older twin sisters Abbie and Beatie showed no signs of any asthmatic tendencies and they were both at school that day.

Abigale need not have worried. The weather held, the baby was in good form and his great-granddad was delighted to see them. He had retired from the pit and was enjoying the first real summer's day of the season. He met them along the lane from his cottage. It was his custom to take a "constitutional" walk in the late morning particularly if the weather was fine. At the sight of the small party approaching he gave out a thunderous shout and raised both arms above his considerable frame in lusty greeting. He gathered his daughter-in-law in one arm and his grand daughter in the other, and peered down at the terrified child as he laughed and asked the women what they had bought in the pushchair then? He hadn't made the acquaintance of this young man before. Releasing the laughing women, he bent down towards the baby who cried immediately at the sight of the enormous man with the big voice and snow white beard. He wore a cap and asked the little chap what he had to cry about? He prodded the little boy's chest with the mouth end of the curled stem pipe that hung from his lips, when it wasn't being used to poke babies in greeting. He picked Len out of his carriage and held him aloft. The height to which he was suddenly hoisted immediately caused him to stop crying ..... probably from fear! It was the first test for his great-granddad's powerful arms in Len's experience and the start of a long and respectful association between the oldest and youngest members of the "clan". The old chief was a kind and generous man, although he had a reputation for not suffering fools lightly. He didn't surrender ground to anyone – least of all his sons, who, when they were young, were expected to "toe the line" ..... or receive his toe.

The cottage was idyllic. It lived, on the very side of Wasson Pool. He was a lucky man to be given the tenancy of it when made Manager of the pit, and he knew it. He liked nothing better than to be sitting at the side of the pool, smoking his pipe in the company of any of his large, growing and well spread family. It was the norm to have large families and each family seemed to have the tragedy of an infant death to live with. Life had been tough in so many ways but he had made a good job of it, he thought. He had been lucky enough to avoid the massacres of the World War by being too old for call-up. His job had been essential to the war effort. He would not have been called up anyway – even if his age had been right. He could have volunteered mind –, as did many of his friends and some of the younger chaps in the family. Mining was tough – but it was regular and he had controlled the operation here at Jubilee in his own way – despite his differences with the owners.

The smallholding at the side of the cottage was worked by John Drew's family, some of whom still lived with him. Apart from the produce, they also provided tea and general refreshments. Passing traffic was light. The nearest neighbours were half a mile away and they relied for custom from the men working the pit and the courting couples who found the pool a magnet as a weekend focus. The winding gear at the pit head towered above the boundary hedge spoiling the view towards Hampstead and Great Barr but the views in the other directions were clear to the horizon.

Chapter Seventeen –

NORMALITY

It was the Saturday before Advent Sunday when Len had progressed to the point where he could be allowed home for the first time since the accident on the 23rd July 1972. Progress had been slow by his own standards. He was still relying heavily on the wheelchair. There was no prospect of him being able to get upstairs to bed. Brenda had organised a bed in the ground floor lounge for him in their well ordered and tidy semi-detached in Halesowen. It was good to have him home. It was good not to have to travel to Oswestry several times a week. She knew that it would only be a temporary stay but it marked progress that at one time seemed beyond the reach even of someone with Len's spirit. Brenda, accompanied by Irene Rudge, a neighbour from the houses opposite, got Len to church at St Hilda's on Advent Sunday and the Reverend Jack Piggott gave them a particularly warm welcome. He altered the service to include "Love Divine" in the list of hymns, especially for Len. Christmas was different that year but at least they were blessed to spend the time together – and at home.

Brenda's employers – GKN – had been particularly understanding. She had been working hours that were very much of her own choosing since the accident and this had helped her remain sane, if permanently worn out. She hated having to rely on relatives and friends who had been so good to her and Len by ferrying her to hospital. Brother Ray and Brother-in law Derek had been particularly helpful and Les Postlethwaite, a fellow parishioner, had always been happy to help out.

She could not drive herself. She had taken the test some years before but had failed on the first attempt. She was annoyed when she failed because she felt she had been close. Just one item on which she had not come up to standard..... and the man gave her the pink slip! At the time there was almost no chance of having her own car and she had not applied to re-test. "How times change," she thought to herself so many times during the dark nights from August 1972 through the depths of winter and into February 1973. It was on just such a dark night in February when she was not due to visit the hospital, that she phoned Len. She was overflowing with good news. She was able to tease him that something great had happened that day. Len grappled with the portent of what she had to tell him; so she kept him waiting ..... just a little longer..... to enhance the delicious moment. At last ..... she spilled the beans. She had passed the test that afternoon. She was bringing mother and Len's mother to see him at the weekend. It was a rare moment of sunshine in their grey winter. Her delight was infectious and it kept them both buoyed, until she drove through the hospital gates, of her own volition, for the first time. She was right to think it was of immediate help to her but she had no idea of the value it would be in the future.

About a month later Len was given the news for which he had been waiting years. Or so it seemed to him. Could it only have been eight months since his admission? He was to go home. It was March 1973. He vowed early after his admission, that he would walk out of the hospital and so, he did. He was aided by crutches and the pull on his arms was colossal. With the strength he had built into his upper body and virtually no use at all in the legs, he was able to swing himself along for quite a considerable distance. The corridors serving the different wards, if laid end to end, would probably have stretched for half a mile and he had assiduously practised his painstaking walk along them in fair weather and foul. He could have sat back and become an invalid forever but he wasn't made that way. He had set himself targets all his life. He was used to meeting them. His ambition to walk from the ward, was, to date, the most difficult to achieve because of the ravages he had undergone mentally as well as physically.

But he achieved it.

Brenda was there to drive him. He wanted no ambulance. He wanted no alterations to the house. He wanted no ramps. Brenda smiled to herself. He *was* getting better. "That's the man I married! That's my old Len!"

Watching him refusing any help in his efforts to get up the step and into the house on that first occasion, would have convinced anyone of sound mind that he would never be able to negotiate the stairs. What on earth was he thinking about, not wanting a stairlift, not wanting ramps? Had the accident affected his balance? Of his mind that is? In the colloquial idiom, had he gone yampy?

His family and long time cohorts knew him far better than that. They knew that his resolve would make the best of any situation. He was used to pushing his body to the limit and beyond in his running and climbing and he was in the business of doing it again. He had embarked on a whole new way of life, full of challenge. He had always thrived on challenge.

He had confounded his rescuers, he confounded the Swiss doctors and he confounded doctors and nursing staff at Oswestry,

Friends and family are only surprised when he is not confounding them.

He had to be patient but patience was not one of his strong points. That is probably why he had risen in his chosen career to the point where he was chief design draughtsman at Kaye Alloy Castings, part of a famous heavy industrial group of companies. He was used to working under pressure and getting the job done! He had lots of career left in front of him when the accident happened. He was determined to get back to work, just as he was determined to get to the top of the stairs at home. Those were his immediate goals. "Immediate" had taken on a different value since the accident. It meant "as soon as possible" in practice, although it is true to say the "goals" were immediate. "As soon as possible", was a matter of eighteen months before Len was able to master the stairs. He got to the top at last and since then he has slept in the same bedroom for the past twenty-nine years. Going to bed at night and getting himself down in the morning. He washes, shaves, dresses without help and all the time he needs to support himself with some form of crutch when he is standing. He drives his own specially adapted car to venues and holidays all over the United Kingdom and covers more than an "average" mileage every year!

Chapter Eighteen –

SMALL TALK

Len had been a member of the choir at St Hilda's Church Warley since he was eight years old. At the time of his accident and for some time afterwards, the vicar at church was The Reverend J D Piggott. He was most supportive of Len and Brenda and their families during the darkest of their days and during the initial period of convalescence and recovery. Len wanted to get back to Church. Very early on after returning home he was able to resume his place near the Altar at St Hilda's. His tenor voice was rusty but still strong and a few practices brought him back into good singing condition. All part of the recovery. He was sure that the exercise of the vocal chords was good for his chest. He was forty-six years old and still felt vulnerable to chest infections, as he had in his childhood.

It was after a choir practice, one night, Len found that the usual chat and banter had developed into a cross-examination of his experience, particularly from the younger members of the choir. He had gone over the ground several times in his discussions with members of the West Bromwich Mountaineering Club. They had also been so supportive. Members of the family and friends also wanted to know the full details. Gradually, a pattern was developing so that he found himself automatically dropping into a familiar routine when anyone prompted him with a question that may have betrayed more than a surface or passing interest. He never did have too much difficulty talking and suddenly he became aware that other people, apart from himself, were interested in him. They were interested in not only what happened to him on the 23rd July 1972, but also what had happened since. Why he still made the effort to go to church when it was easier to stay at home? He certainly had the best reason in the world for not going to choir practice, if he should chose to use it, they told him.

What Len probably failed to notice at this stage, was that not only did his story stand up on it's own as a good yarn but he had an engaging and wonderfully humorous way of putting it across to people. Even more esoteric to Len, perhaps, was the enthusiasm that came across from the speaker. The love of the mountains. The regard he had for others, his own commitment and people like him, fellow climbers. The fervour and the re-affirmation of his enduring and deep-seated faith with which he sprinkled the fascinating facts. His stiff upper-lip "Britishism" in an international arena. These combined to present his audience with rich entertainment.

It made an impact on one youthful choir member. The following week he asked Len if he would be good enough to go to his father's "club" one night and give them a talk. For sure the youngster had sold Len as being "worth a try" to his father.

It transpired that the boy's father was a member of 'Rotary'. It was a regular feature of their meetings that a guest speaker would be provided to address them on any subject that would provide some measure of interest for the members. Len hadn't considered the possibility.

He didn't really want this, but he had been caught off guard by this forward young man. Len would admit to being privately taken aback and at the same time, just a trifle flattered at the thought that this young man and his father had decided between them that it was worth the effort.

And so it came to pass. He had a few slides to illustrate the talk but they were uninspiring. "This is how I climbed the Matterhorn in 1971 and this is how I climbed it in 1972" he thought to himself. Who is going to buy that as entertainment?

"I wasn't able to get a shot of myself falling off!"

"Now," he thought, "that's sounding more like it!" He had no equipment to show the slides, no entertainment, no prepared talk and no track record in delivering public speeches, so he went along and entertained the members of Rotary. Thus began the most rich and in some ways, the most rewarding time of his life. A series of tales, co-incidences, and enrichment of faith that all add up to a 'miracle' for Len.

He borrowed equipment, he gave some thought to a script but abandoned the idea of having to trail notes around with him. He knew enough about it to talk to people without notes! He enlisted the help of stalwarts like his brother, David and his brother-in-law, Brian Pate, to take him and assist with the technical operations – his roadies!

The first talk spawned another, then another, and on it went. Shortly after the first series of talks he received a request to give a talk to the Church at Boldmere St Michael's, Sutton Coldfield, where the vicar was ....The Reverend J D Piggott.

At first Len was genuinely short of confidence in himself, although anyone who had known him for sometime, would be convinced that he was well equal to the job of entertaining! At times, he found it demoralising to sit in the car, in the dark, outside a venue unknown to him, with people inside waiting for his talk. He would rather have gone home!

Before his first talk he wrote to Ruth Brozy, seeking moral support. He asked her to tell him what to say. She responded by return of post, telling him that he had said it all in his letters to her. She could not improve on what he had told her. If he felt short of material he should quote Psalm 121. She was still a wellspring of inspiration to both Len and Brenda. Her regular correspondence still helped the healing process.

He need not have doubted his ability to cope with the situations that cropped up before the audiences. He was invariably met by people who could not do enough for him, before he even reached the audience. The sight of the maimed figure swinging himself slowly, painfully on to the stage had the audience immediately on his side. Then the sidelong, impish grin would hold the audience for a moment before he said, "Are you feeling sorry for me?" He always got at least one response of "Yes," and this enabled him to continue "Well don't, because you are looking at the happiest man in the world!" Quite an opening for a man who can't walk without his crutches.

The audience was his.

Then he would explain that because he was paralysed. Because he had broken his neck between the sixth and seventh vertebrae, he felt no pain from the chest down. Except, occasionally, in the extremities of his arms and legs. He therefore felt good, he loved mountains and that is what he had come to talk to them about. God had given him the experience necessary and the will to do it. That's why he was "The happiest man in the world!"

Chapter Nineteen –

SCOTLAND

After the first few talks, Len realised that this was what he wanted to do. It was no cheap introduction to say that he was the happiest man in the world. He *was* the happiest man in the world in that privileged environment. He grew in strength and found that what he was saying in the course of his talk, whether it be for half-an-hour or two hours, was inspirational to many in his audience. What an amazing transformation in his outlook in the course of a few short months. He had found his new *niche* in life. God really was with him, as he always had been. In the depths of his despair, in his fall from the mountain, in his happiest moments. He was there!

The talks were taking over more and more of his time. Simultaneously he was learning to be more independent and self-reliant. There were and there would always be some things he could not do and he accepted this. Brenda says that she did not realise she had a disabled husband until she retired. He grew to such a state of independence that it was not until she was with him for long periods of the day that she established a pattern to his disability. How he coped on his own when she worked for twenty-five years after his accident will always be something of a mystery to her.

It was about this time that Len learned of the accident to the son of Francis Jones. Francis was the Senior Consultant for spinal injuries at the Oswestry hospital, the very hospital that had helped to breathe new life into his battered frame. The young man had been involved in a serious car accident and had been admitted to the hospital with major spinal injuries.

The irony of the situation hit Len hard. This surgeon with the power to heal and who had put that power to such productive use in so many cases, particularly in Len's case, was now facing the prospect of having his beloved son needing care at an advanced level. It was reported that the young man's spirit was brilliant, however, and that surely must help his father to bear the pressure. Treating patients who are strangers presents certain problems but no doubt having to administer to one's own close family members must present a totally different and more difficult challenge.

*   *   *   *   *

Things kept happening for Len. As early as September 1973; only six months after leaving the Oswestry hospital complete with wheelchair, Brenda decided that it was time for both of them to get back to their favourite "together" haunt. It had not seemed possible to Len when he left Oswestry that he would ever get back to Scotland; yet in such short span he was loaded into their car, Brenda at the wheel, and a tour of the Cairngorms was under way. They called on their old friends, Dennis and Pat Rosenfield at Loch Morlich, Marie Ewan at Braemar and Tom Wilson at Aviemore. The trip acted as a great tonic for them both. For Len it was a signpost that pointed to more than a "cabbage" existence. For Brenda it was a completely new experience because she had not previously had even to think about her husband's welfare. She used to find it difficult to keep up with him so she had got into the habit of not even trying at times. It was her wont to 'let him go' when he became imbued with a wish to get into some new challenge of physical endurance. "Some of your more scatter-brained ideas", she would throw at him. Life's ironies were to hang particularly heavily on the shoulders of each of them in the early years of Len's incapacity. Perhaps the biggest of all was Brenda's tendency to want to attempt a little more in the way of climbing than she had ever contemplated when Len was so super-fit. It was a gradual trait. Did it happen because he was so fit that he hadn't the patience to wait for her? She never would attempt anything remotely dangerous but there is no doubt that her own interest in the mountainous areas of the world was enhanced. The magnetic draw of the wild was working it's magic, ever so slowly, on Brenda. Len's enthusiasm for it was never to diminish. Just the opposite in fact!

Over the next few years Len's prowess as a lecturer became something of a byword in the circles close to him. The West Bromwich Mountaineering Club, local scout groups, Church Groups of all denominations and facets (Mothers Union, WI, Choirs, Clubs male, female and mixed) were warming to this mature man with the face of a youth, the enthusiasm of a successful football supporters club, the physical restrictions of the paraplegic and the impish smile of the choirboy. His visits to Scotland with Brenda were an annual pilgrimage. Each time he was able to achieve something new, his talks became the richer for it. His photography, always of a near professional standard, became more polished. His talks were extended from the story of the fall, to provide a second string to his bow in the form of a talk on Scotland. This was useful when he had to pay a third and fourth visit to the same venue – it gave him a few more options to keep the audience interested.

He hardly needed to have concerned himself. His audience would be there to greet him even if he had nothing new to tell them! He would say, for instance, that he had just been on a visit to the Oswestry Unit to talk to a young man who had fallen from a kitchen stool and suffered similar problems to himself. His deep feeling for the young man would penetrate to all in the hall as he told them of the patient's problems. Then he would wait for the hush to descend and grab the moment by the scruff of the neck. "That illustrates exactly what I have said for years" – he would wait a second – "If you're going to have an accident – HAVE A GOOD ONE!"

The spell was broken. The audience was laughing again. Not at the hapless young man's position. Far from it. They were laughing with Len – at Len – when he followed up with "How could I stand here and tell you a story about how I fell off the kitchen stool! It wouldn't last more than ten seconds. I've been talking to you for an hour and the helicopter hasn't arrived yet!" His sacrifice of physical dexterity was being replaced slowly by a mastery of timing, of verbal delivery. Not that he was ever known to be sluggish in that direction!

The audience knew that he could have delivered an amusing. hour long, lecture on something as mundane as "making a cup of tea", if he set his mind to it.

It was taking a long time but as the years progressed and as Len appreciated the effect he had when he was talking to people, he became more convinced that his life had taken on this pattern by design. It was becoming something of a miracle to him that he had survived his accident, that he had become stronger in so many ways since the fall, that he was gradually becoming physically more able to cope with his disability and, *God Bless Her*, that Brenda was so wonderfully supportive. What he did not know at that time was that forces were at work that were to further shape the jigsaw of the miracle.

Chapter Twenty –

FLYING VISIT

Len learned to drive again, in a vehicle converted to accommodate all controls on the steering wheel, or very close to it. He became proficient at driving the car. No doubt this was because he was as determined to conquer that problem as he was with all the other challenges that came his way!

In 1979 he decided it was time for him to take Brenda to Scotland again – just as he had when they had the Claude-Butler tandem. This time he would be providing all the power, despite his seventy-five percent permanent disability. This percentage was eclipsed only by an almost one hundred percent experience of good weather when they visited Scotland. This particular visit began to look true to form as they approached the Scottish border from the direction of Carlisle. The skies cleared and, on their way to Harwick they decided to fulfil one of their long held ambitions. It was particularly important to Brenda. They would call on Tom and Marta Robinson *en route* to the Cairngorm!

This couple had been particularly supportive of Brenda in 1972. Taking dinner, alone, in the hotel at Berne, Brenda was contemplating the enormity of the events of the previous few days. She tried to imagine life without her husband or life with a husband who would be so different from the powerhouse that she had married. At that time, it was almost impossible to perceive Len following a life beyond the confines of a hospital. On that particular evening of despair, in the quiet that accompanied the ordeal of trying to eat food again, Brenda listened absently to the conversation at the next table for some minutes before realising that it was being conducted in English. The couple had finished their meal, when, with uncharacteristic nerve, Brenda stopped at their table and enquired what sort of day they had enjoyed. The complement was returned and in no time, Brenda was

113

recounting the situation in which she found herself. The words had flooded out! There was no place for her normal reticence in this situation. They needed to spill out and they did!

Thus began another close relationship with this Scottish pair. So important to the recuperation of both Brenda and Len. Marta and Tom had shared the visiting at the hospital in those now distant days, with the legendary Ruth Brozy and Brenda. They proved to be a source of warm strength and comfort to Brenda and an inspiration to Len. None of them would have dared to contemplate at that time, the possibility of the impaired couple being able to undertake a journey of three hundred miles, Len at the wheel, seven years later. This time it was Len and Brenda who were on something of a mercy mission. Tom was in his eighty-fifth year and the last communication from Marta had reported that he had lost his sight. It was with an air of slight trepidation they stood at the door of the Scottish couple's home. The tension was immediately dispelled with the obvious joy on the face of Marta when she opened the door to them. "How lovely to see you both" she said and, without taking another breath, "Tom is next door watching the football match on television between Scotland and England!"

She sensed the hesitance on the part of her visitors at this remark. She explained that Tom's miracle had occurred when a newly perfected operation had been completed on her husband to restore his eyesight. Len reflected that it was a double miracle that he was able to accompany Brenda to their beloved Scotland and that Tom was able to see them for himself. It was a rewarding experience for the couple who owed so much to Marta and Tom and had the effect of setting their holiday off on the best possible footing.

For reasons best known to him alone, Len had set himself the goal of reaching the top of Cairngorm. This is a climb that eludes the majority of fit people. Len had practised on his elbow crutches for the previous seven years but even by his standards, the ambition was puzzling. He put it down to the possibility of using the chairlift to a height of 3600 feet – but that still left a tricky climb for him. As they approached from the Tomintoul Road the eastern slopes of the Cairngorms slowly unmasked a good layer of snow still lying, even as late as the 28th of May and his ambition took a decided knock.

Brenda returned home on Wednesday 2nd June 1979. Her mother was unwell and she needed to get back to her. Len was left to his own devices from that day. He drove Brenda to the station at Aviemore so that she could return home by train. It was the first time that he had been away from Brenda for any length of time in almost seven years. The parting at Aviemore was preceded with a long list of well-intentioned instructions to her husband. At his protestation Brenda countered with, "Well you may have forgotten but I haven't! Last time I left you to your own devices you broke your neck. Remember?"

He was still chuckling from the pointed intent of the last ironic remark as the train gathered speed on its journey south. It was at this point that the loneliness of his situation hit him between the eyes. There was something of the old boyish excitement stirring in him as he contemplated his immediate future. Life was here to be lived for him...... by him..... for a while..... on his own. The window of the Nevis Sports shop in Aviemore was a magnet. The train had left the station barely minutes before, as Len stared at the modern clothing and up-to-date ironmongery for climbers that lay, apparently carelessly scattered across the window enclosure. To catch a Len? Not quite. He realised that with the snow on the tops and the standard problems he had to deal with, any more climbing was ruled out for this holiday!

What did arrest his attention, was a poster in the window, advertising gliding at the Cairngorm Gliding Club. Could he? Should he?

Len and Brenda's luck with the weather in Scotland was phenomenal. He could not remember a holiday north of the border that had been spoilt by rain, and this holiday was the twenty-fifth spent in the company of the whisky makers. He made his way to the side of Loch Morlich, faced the white-topped Cairngorms reflecting in the water against the clear blue sky, alone, happy and completely at peace.

*   *   *   *   *

The following morning Len went through the complicated process of washing and dressing with a tingle of excitement even more marked than usual. Every day was a bonus to him but that day promised to eclipse the norm because he had decided he would visit the gliding club – just to have a look! So it was with more gusto than usual that he negotiated the stairs down to the breakfast room at Mullingarroch, only to be greeted with the sad news that Mrs Grant, the landlady, had just been told of her father's death. After breakfast all the guests would obviously have to leave, and yet with all her problems she wanted to phone round her friends to ensure Len would be adequately housed. By sheer chance, Brenda phoned at 8.30 a.m. that morning, "Just to see how Len was coping?" as she said. "You must come home Len," her concern showing.

"What? Not on your life!" was his predictable reply. "What would the doctors and physiotherapists at Oswestry say if I gave in to a minor challenge like this?" This was precisely the type of occasion that paraplegics and tetraplegics had been taught to deal with by the staff on Len's regular visits to Oswestry since his discharge from the hospital six years earlier. "The weather is wonderful! I shall cope!" he told Brenda. His enthusiasm was less than convincing and she wondered why she had bothered to phone him. It would only serve to cast a shadow over the rest of the day for her.

No shadow was allowed to impose itself on Len's plans and he had forgotten to tell Brenda of his proposed visit to the gliding club!

From Mullingarroch Farm, he decided to drive up Glen More to Loch Morlich Youth hostel. He had used the hostel many times in the seventeen years prior to his accident, sometimes with Brenda, sometimes with friends from the West Bromwich Mountaineering Club. He was delighted to find Dennis Rosenfield still in charge at the hostel. Dennis's reaction was quite predictable – he would be delighted to show Len that the hostel could look after the disabled just as well as the fit! Dennis's wife Patricia produced the finest food that Len had ever been served, even in his wide experience of Scotland. A rare treat not extended to all youth hostellers.

*   *   *   *   *

Len sat in his car, watching the activities at the gliding club. The winching of the gliders into the air and the landings were fascinating to him. After a short while a man strolled over to talk and asked Len if he would be interested in a flight. "You bet I would," was Len's reply. "But I have got one or two problems," he said, indicating the disabled controls of the car and his elbow crutches lying on the seat next to him. "I have been watching the operators climbing in and out of the machines and it would be impossible for me to get into one of them."

"Impossible?" The stranger rolled the word around his mouth, pushed his tongue into his cheek, and repeated reflectively. "Impossible? That's a big word. How heavy are you? Can you make your way to the glider over there?"

"I am nine stone seven and the answer to your last question is 'Yes'," Len replied with a renewed sense of "lift off" exciting the feeling parts of his upper body. Understandably he was asked to sign a disclaimer in the event of accident. He couldn't sign fast enough! He made his way slowly, and to the watching group, painfully, over to the two-seater glider. John, a powerfully built young man, picked Len up like a babe in arms and gently lowered him into the cockpit. He strapped him securely into the seat, replaced the canopy and they were ready. A man named Alan introduced himself as pilot, climbed into the rear seat, went through the routine checks and tested the signals. The winch took up the slack. Suddenly the green airstrip rushed towards him as the glider accelerated, they were airborne and climbing rapidly. A bump beneath his seat told him the cable had detached and they were completely free of motive power.

The thrill experienced by Len, particularly as he had negotiated his own way into the flight, was more rewarding than he dared dream. The freedom of the noiseless flight above Glen Feshie with the mighty Cairngorm range, snow-clad and to his left, was an experience that will stay with him forever. The fact that the flight was only timed to last for ten minutes was the only disappointment. Could he come back tomorrow? He wondered!

Back at the hostel, he was in time to be invited by Dennis to "sit-in" on a talk that the warden was giving to a group of school students in residence for a couple of nights. The accent was on "safety", and Dennis thought Len's presence would be helpful! The newly recruited glider fan was pleased that so many of the climbs and walks covered by Dennis were areas that he knew very well from the number of times he had visited them before his accident. He referred to the Shelter Stone, Ben Macdui, Loch Avon, Loch Etchachan and Lairig Ghru.

All places visited by Len in the past, some of them on several different occasions. How unusual for Len to be sitting listening to the talk with slide-show, rather than to be the person conducting matters.

After breakfast the following day, Len called at the shop attached to the Cairngorm tea rooms where the lady behind the counter was pleased to load a new film into his camera. Fortified in two senses, he pointed his car toward the gliding club and was greeted like an old friend by the crew. They were operating as "ground crew" again when he arrived and promptly insisted that he should join them for coffee. Whilst imbibing the hot caffeine from mugs as big as buckets, they invited Len to his second flight. He would happily have stayed all day with them, drinking coffee, basking in the warm sunshine, swapping stories and generally being glad to be alive. Soon it was his turn. He was lifted easily into the cockpit and in no time was up in the blue, blue sky in a silence that was so quiet, he found it quite spooky. Alan's voice bought music to his ears as the pilot announced, "Len, yesterday was your training flight. Today we will do some real flying!" He turned the silent silver bird towards the Cairngorm, in search of the rising thermals that would help them fly above the mountaintops. Below, Len could make out, etched into the hillside, a well-defined track that he identified as the path leading to the cairn on top of Stob Ban More. Winding its way through the glen, a silver thread reflected the sunlight, tracing the course of the River Feshie. The dwellings of Aclean could be made out on the left bank, whilst Feschie Lodge stood in splendid isolation on the opposite side.

They flew over Loch Einich and the brightly coloured sails of the yachts far below could have been toy boats in a bath. Alan's voice from behind told Len to spot the caravan hidden between the pine trees to his left. "That is where I am living at the moment." Len felt a sharp tug at his heartstrings as he shouted back, scarcely able to disguise a chuckle, "Some people have all the luck!" With such beautiful surroundings, the water, trees and a major range of mountains forming the backcloth it was difficult to envisage anything more idyllic. It seemed that Alan was as keen a mountaineer as Len and although it was clear that he enjoyed the company of his gliding friends, Alan was glad to have someone with him who appreciated the magnificence of the mountains even more than did Alan himself.

Len's enthusiasm was boundless as he spotted one familiar landmark after another, far different in aspect from what he was used to, but in some ways, "More exciting for a' that," he quipped to his Scottish friend. He was a child again.....Charles Leonard York was enjoying himself more than at any time since his fall. He never dreamed that he would be able to take part in any outdoor activity on that scale..... but the real thrill was yet to come! The altimeter was pointing to just below 3000 ft when he looked down into Glen Einich where the sheer walls of the corrie disappeared into the depths of the loch. Through the perspex dome of the aircraft he saw the peaks of Braeriach, Cairntoul, Angel's Peak and Ben Macdui. The great gash of the Lairig Ghru knifed its way through the mass of the mountains, splitting the Cairngorms into two distinct parts. It was a 1" Ordnance Survey Map without the contour lines. The glider circled and the compass pointed westward to the familiar shape of Ben Nevis in the distance. This sparked further animated reminiscences from both flyers.

The trip lasted one hour and the excited "little boy" passenger had matured into a well-educated and strangely humbled adult, by the intoxication of his second gliding experience.

Chapter Twenty-One –

TENT LIFE

It was early summer 1980 when Dave Munslow asked if Len would like to accompany him, his younger brother, Geoff, and Keith O'Rielly, on a visit to the Alps. The visit would take in The Eiger at Kleine Sheidegg and ....Zermatt. The name still had a magic for Len. It took him about five seconds to formulate a half-choked "Yes please!" David and Geoff owned a camping equipment and outdoor pursuits shop in Halesowen and Len was a regular caller, keeping in touch with developments in the climbing world. He would probably have to cancel one or two talks but he would make sure the organisers of the venues would understand that he was only postponing them – he could add to the content of the talks after travelling to Zermatt again. The only thing he would miss which couldn't be repeated was the fiftieth wedding anniversary of Aunt May and Uncle Bill. Uncle Bill was one of his late mother's five brothers. It was inconsiderate of them to arrange it for a date when he would be in Zermatt! As he explained to them in a letter of apology, they really were a much loved pair of relatives and nothing, but nothing other than a trip to Zermatt would have caused him to miss such an important date in his calendar. Len's letter was read out by Bill's son Brian, at the function and it was so well worded that a spontaneous round of applause greeted the reading. The room was full of Len's relatives. Brenda was there in person, and if he had any reservations he need not have done so. Everyone wished him well on his return trip to Zermatt, delighted that he had been spared to make the trip. Delighted also, that he had the strength of character to undertake it while still so seriously disabled.

Early in September 1980 Len was once again occupying his own small mountain tent in the Swiss Alps. His phenomenal luck with the weather continued. Switzerland had a poor summer that year, along with most of Europe. Autumn promised well and he was there to enjoy it! He found that progress was slow in the evenings to crawl into the tent, with virtually no movement in his lower limbs. He then squeezed himself into his sleeping bag and then faced the enormous problem of pulling up the zip to retain the body heat. Even in good weather, it is cold lying on the ground, at altitude, in September. The whole operation took about half-an-hour. In the mornings, he found it helpful to rise about one hour before his friends, so that they would all be ready at the same time. They occupied separate tents, so he did not have to disturb them. Dressing was particularly difficult, lying flat on his back, in the confined space and only able to wriggle!

Most of the nights were spent in the tent but he did have the luxury of a hotel when the rest of the team was to be away for two nights, climbing on the Eiger. Even so, Len rose at 05.30 hrs to sit with the glass doors to his room wide open while he filmed the sun rising over the Wetterhorn, to his left. The north face of the Eiger looked calm and uninhabited at that time of day but by 07.30 he could see four or five black dots on the lower snowfield of the Eiger's West flank. He knew it was his friends, with others, who had left their bivvies and were on their way to another unforgettable day's climbing.

They spent two good days at Kleine Sheidegg before boarding the train to Grund. They picked up their car from the car park and were *en route* again to Zermatt. They left Grindelwald in good weather but by the time they reached Tasch, below Zermatt, rain and low cloud had spoilt the record for weather. Tents were pitched for the night while the elements were still distinctly inclement. It was much the same next morning but it promised to be better at Zermatt and the party took a chance. The approach to the cable car serving the Klein Matterhorn is steep, even to fit mountaineers and it necessitated a "carry" from his friends to transport Len the last fifty yards. They utilised his elbow crutches as a makeshift "seat" and soon the cable car was accelerating up through the clouds. Suddenly the world was in sunshine again as the machinery whisked the party silently upwards. The blue sky framed snow-covered peaks all around them. To the right, the Matterhorn stood proud and alone, it's peak pointing like the spire of a giant cathedral towards the heavens. The summit was bright and shining in the sunlight whilst the bottom was lost in dark, boiling cloud.

Len found the sight of the fatalistic mountain an experience so moving that even he was not quite prepared for it and his eyes stayed riveted to it until the cable car stopped at the Trockner Steg intermediate station.

Len said goodbye to his friends at this point so that they could concentrate on their own ambitions for the day. He dearly wanted to complete the last part of the journey on his own. He stayed for two hours at Trockner Steg so that he could become acclimatised to the height for the final lift to the top. The stage had been newly opened in February of that year and by September five people had died from heart attacks either on the cable car, or once they reached the top. It completes the journey to 13,000ft at a remarkably swift pace in deceptively comfortable conditions and Len tried to anticipate possible problems, particularly bearing in mind his still limited locomotion. On disembarking from the car a 200 metre tunnel separates the traveller from the plateau. Len made his way, on his crutches, 20 metres at a time, the journey punctuated by a stop for a few minutes each time. Never was he made to feel so acutely aware as his body reminded him that only one of his lungs functioned. This particular part of the journey often makes normally fit people stop to catch their breath and faintings are frequent. He persevered and at last he came to the end of the tunnel. He stood for a moment, making sure his light reflecting lenses were in place and testing his grip on his crutches before stepping from the gloom of the tunnel into the brilliance of the snow covered vista that stretched for about a mile and a half before him. No words have been coined that could begin to explain the depth of feeling, the supreme elation, the very breath of God that touched Len's face at that moment.

He had returned!

The Matterhorn itself is hidden as one emerges from the tunnel and to get into position for a good view of that mountain, entails a traverse of about 50 metres to the right. So Len, on his crutches, made certain the tip of each one was firmly anchored in the snow before each movement. Swinging his legs and "skating" the soles along the powdered snow that had been "tamped" into a firm base by skiers, he made his careful way to the point where he could photograph the mountain.

He was at once cross that the steel "hawser" ropes spoiled the view and simultaneously thankful for the part they played in making the whole journey possible. The hawsers support the machinery that makes the journey possible at all. An engineering marvel, even by the exceptional standards of the Continental engineers who build these remarkable people carriers, in the most inhospitable places.

He knew he had more than God to thank for delivering him to this magnificent place. He took a moment to say a prayer of thanks that included all the members of 'his team'. The doctors, surgeons, hospital staff, his rescuers, family and friends.

What of Brenda? How does one start to thank her? As he took in the view which is so reminiscent of the panorama from the top of the Matterhorn itself, he was aware of Brenda. It was as if she were there with him. Perhaps one day she would be. He felt so close to her.

He said quietly "Thankyou Brenda"

Such a long way from Clent.

*   *   *.   *   *

Half an hour at the top of Klein Matterhorn was long enough for Len, particularly as he was alone. His "platform in the sky" was left to the trippers and skiers as he returned, via cable car, to Zermatt. His camera was full of record, his memories poignant, his heart full and his body completely exhausted.

The following day was sun-drenched again, enabling their programme to take a similar pattern. His friends left him at Zermatt cable car station to pursue their climbs while Len, acclimatised by the previous day's excursion, felt strong enough to tackle the trip up to Swarzee alone.

The Swarzee route is the cable car that drops its passengers at a height of about 10,000 ft. It is the closest one can get to the summit of the Matterhorn by mechanical assistance, apart from helicopter. In typical Alpine tradition, it has a restaurant, tables, chairs and benches where mountaineers and day-trippers rub shoulders. The former fortify themselves for the climbs ahead, the latter just enjoy the views.

On that day in September 1980, Len sat on a bench with his back to the Matterhorn; his gaze fixed on the distant Monte Rosa. It is a Mountain in Italy and it looks like an iced cake! Just as it did on the day when Len and some friends climbed to it's summit in 1971. The first alpine peak in his bag. So innocuous did it look from his vantage point but he knew what a sting the mountain has in it's tail. The last 500-ft is a knife-edge ridge covered in snow and cornices.

He turned and put the binoculars on the Matterhorn. This took him to the activity of the Hornli Hut at about 12000-ft, but he had difficulty locating the Solvay Hut, higher still. He had no difficulty locating the very spot where he had fallen and while the sun still shone with a burning heat, he could not help feeling an involuntary shudder across his shoulders.

Swarzee is one of the best tourist sites in the Alps. It is a magnet, to climber and sightseer alike. Few people visit Zermatt without visiting Swarzee. On that particular day, Len had time on his hands and it became clear that many people were walking past, looking at the crippled figure sitting on the bench, alone, with his crutches. They couldn't resist the temptation to ask permission to sit beside him and get to the subject of "How the hell have you got up here?" They could not be asking a more authoritative person. They were regaled with information about the Matterhorn, fed snippets of the dangers and told the story of the fall and the recovery. So practised was Len of course with the tongue that it was never long before a small crowd gathered. The paralysis never did affect his mouth!

In no time at all and much to his embarrassment, he had earned about twenty Swiss francs as tourists insisted on pushing notes into his hand "To have a Drink with them!" He decided to call it a day and return to Zermatt before one of the "tourists" turned out to be a tax inspector.

They made their way back home the following day and as they passed through Dover Len was glad that he did not have to declare any more broken limbs. He was so grateful to Dave, Geoff and Keith for the way that had fed him, pitched tents for him and done so much to make his holiday comfortable. He wondered how many physically capable people would want to be hampered by a 75% disabled person on a round trip of 1700 miles. For them it was a journey into the unknown. They were magnificent!

*   *   *   *   *

A few days after returning from the trip, Len's story was run as an article in the "Sunday Express" by Sally Staples and the "Daily Telegraph" obviously picked it up. A letter dated 19th September 1980 dropped through Len's letterbox a few days later, it had come from an address in Hampshire. "I don't think I know anyone in Hampshire," thought Len as he looked at the hand-written letter. It read:

19th September 1980

"Dear Mr York,

I have read a most interesting article in the Daily Telegraph and admire your courage after your accident. My Great-Uncle Whymper was leader of the first team to climb the Matterhorn as you will know. I always find a picture of the mountain is an inspiration, although I am not a mountaineer myself.

With all good wishes
Yours truly,

Whymper Bryan"

Chapter Twenty-Two –

TEN YEARS TO CHAMONIX

Two years later, by September 1982, Dave and Geoff had recovered sufficiently from the first trip to the Alps, to be seduced into thinking they could repeat the journey again. This time they planned to call at Chamonix for a hike up Mont Blanc! They extended the invitation to Len again. Again he accepted without hesitation.

Len reminded everyone that he had started off for Chamonix ten years before and he still hadn't arrived! The route on the map did not appear to need a detour via Grindelwald, Zermatt, Berne, Oswestry, but that was the route fate had decreed.

Glad that the wheels of the car had come to rest on the car deck at Dover, Len found it a relief to stand and stretch the stiffness from his limbs. He felt quite elated at the prospect of getting to the Alps again. "We're well on the way," he thought, as he placed his left stick in front of him and placed all his weight on it, and confidently moved his weight forward. He had assumed the deck was clean and dry. In the half-light of the vehicle deck he could be forgiven for being mistaken. He was again falling at 32 ft per second squared. He and his classmates had learned this all those years previously, but he seemed to have more practical experience of it than most. Not so far did he fall this time as on the famous occasion, but just as quickly. The first contact with the vehicle deck was via the lens of his rimless spectacles as they were pushed back against his head. It seemed to him worse than the fall ten years before as his arms were locked in his elbow crutches and this prevented him from being able to cushion his fall. He passed out as the warmth of the blood filled his right eye.

Geoff was at his side almost instantly as he had heard Len's involuntary, startled shout. He hauled Len to his feet in the confined space between the cars and, wiping away as much blood as possible, pronounced that a three-quarter inch cut above his right eye would need stitching. Len, with customary obduracy, refused to hear of it! He had come to get to Chamonix and that was where he was going! He was not getting off that boat! His friends must have had reservations as they bathed his wound from a tap in the toilet compartment. At last they had made it reasonably clean and against their better judgement, applied antiseptic cream before binding his wound, as tightly as possible, with sticking plaster. Len was grateful that he always wore plastic lenses, or his problems would undoubtedly have been worse. He thanked God that Brenda had not witnessed his fall. She constantly repeated that he was to take things more easily. The boat got under way and soon he wondered if his Maker had forsaken him. The boat was subjected to the worst electrical storm he could remember, as it ploughed it's way toward the French coast in the darkness. Would he ever see Chamonix?

Twenty-four hours later, Len was being chauffeured around the centre of Chamonix in a car with the camping shop logo CASAC on the side. His friends insisted on a circuit of the Jacques Balmat monument to prove to him that they had arrived. The normally omnipresent sight of Mt Blanc was missing. The low cloud was as black as Len's right eye. Within minutes of the car pulling up on the camp site at Les Houches, with perfect timing, the clouds lifted and the sun shone. The first sight of Mont Blanc for Len was a snapshot that he will never forget. As the cloud parted, the sun was low, out of sight of the campers, but it cast a pink glow onto the summit snows and the Aiguille du Midi. The Dru, and the Chamonix Needles slowly unmasked themselves from their shifting wraps.

It was worth the ten-year wait.

Len watched his friends expertly construct their camp in what seemed a twinkling of the eye – a three-man tent complete with safari camp bed and chair for Len's comfort. Feeling inadequate at being only able to watch the proceedings Len told them that the only thing he had to offer in return, was this suddenly wonderful weather. It always accompanied him on trips to both the Alps and Scotland. They agreed it was a fair exchange and they would settle for it as they got behind enormous mugs of tea. They ate a meal cooked on the camp stove, all three of them drinking in the warmth of the dusk. Later, they sat enjoying a glass of the local produce until the part of the sky not occupied by mountains was cloaked in the magic of the Milky Way.

They talked into the early hours of their plans for the following day. Dave and Geoff were to tackle Mont Blanc and Len was to be found a room in a good hotel in Chamonix for a few days. However well they wrapped up the information about their plans it was impossible for them not to notice the wistful look in Len's eye. He was contemplating the experience facing his two friends. They were tackling the permanently white covered mountain for the first time. It had not been a good summer and the weather over the past few days would have contributed to the problems on the mountain. At least there would be a fairly heavy covering of loose snow. It seemed to Len that *he* was the least of their problems. To bring them back to earth he told them that he did not mind them "generally dumping" him, as he carefully worded it, and awaited their pained reaction.

"I shall rely for my survival on my three old friends", Len told them.

"Which friends are these?" asked Dave.

The old sly, sideways smile creased Len's face as he leaned towards them and confided, "My left stick, my right stick and my tongue!"

They feigned raining more blows on his black eye, and turned in for the night still laughing into their sleeping bags.

How true Len's prophecy was to turn out!

*   *   *   *   *

Len's tent was big enough for three fit people. On the safari bed were two sleeping bags. Two, because with his leg and lower limb problems, he was likely to suffer extremes of low temperature in the lower regions during the cold nights. Getting into the gear was a daunting prospect and an operation that took Len the best part of an hour to get himself settled and comfortable. He could hear his companions in the next tent enjoying a mug of something as a nightcap. A pleasure that he denied himself for fear that he would

129

have to get out of the bedding contraption during the night to use the little bottle that accompanied him on these outings. On balance, he decided, it was not worth the effort he might have to make.

The next morning their plans changed. It was decided that they needed a day to acclimatise. Over the early morning cup of tea, it was decided that all three would go to Montenvers on the train. The train climbs up to a point above the "Mer du Glace" giving the brothers a chance to spend a few hours on the glacier and a good spot for Len to view the spectacular scenery from very close quarters.

That's what they thought.

The thick mist, fickle as ever, had returned at the Montenvers level and the superb viewpoint had lost its appeal. "The Dru is just in front of you Len! There, behind the mist, you can almost touch it! The Glacier is over that wall – about three-hundred feet below you!" Dave was doing his best to lighten the disappointment Len was feeling at his first attempt to view these jewels. They sat at fog-laden tables with sunshades, outside the Montenvers Hotel. Each of them knew that the mist could lift in seconds..... but it didn't. The brothers disappeared down the tourist steps to get on to the Glacier and Len took the best part of an hour to finish his pot of tea, before deciding it was time to make a move. He found the personal attention of the stationmaster greatly to advantage as he was escorted to a seat while the other tourists were required to wait their turn in a queue. Len promised the man he would see him again as soon as the weather improved.

*   *   *   *   *

The following day was Wednesday 8th September 1982. Len watched from his open tent door flap as David and Geoff prepared for the attempt to climb Mont Blanc. Len's mood was subdued as he watched them packing snow shovels, sleeping and bivvy bags, ropes, ice-axes, crampons, head torches, emergency rations and spare clothing. Sixty pounds for each man to carry on his back. Any item could prove a lifesaver. Len contrasted the packing that he was doing for his stay at the hotel meanwhile. His lifesavers were his crutches, wallet and camera. Total weight about five pounds. How he wished it could be different!

It took Len no time at all to become acclimatised to the hotel room – although it was on the fifth floor.

He looked round the room. It faced south with large windows opening out onto his own balcony complete with sun-lounger. The view was dominated by the Mont Blanc range. He looked over the balcony to see his two companions waving, just about to move. To relieve his utter frustration, he shouted down to them "Who in their right minds wants to climb Mont Blanc in such hot sunny weather – now I know you're mad!" He didn't think they could hear him, but he was just as sure they would know exactly what he had bellowed at them. 'Yorkie' was full of advice, but this time they paid no heed.

It was always like this, he thought, whenever he sent friends on their way. A sinking wave of frustration, despair, desolation, would overtake him. The loneliness of his situation hit him hard as he sat on the edge of the bed. He was in a strange town, in a country with which he was not good at communicating as he had paid insufficient attention to his French lessons at school. He had serious locomotion problems. "Oh God, please help!" he prayed "You've never let me down yet. Please don't start now. Show me what I should do!" It did not occur to him that he was pushing his arms into his rucksack straps even as he prayed. It did not matter that just to be in Chamonix was a miracle for him. He always sought that extra goal. Now he was here, how could he capitalise? Do something special. A memory for the rest of his life. The opportunities, for a lover of the outdoors, are boundless in a town like "Sham".

He found himself back down in hotel reception without remembering how he got there, although no alcohol had passed his lips that day. He was just about to push the entrance doors open with his stick, when a voice behind him said, "Hello – let me do that for you." He was almost brushed aside by a smiling, attractive young woman who held the door and made as if to support his elbow as he negotiated the first step. "No thanks" said Len, "I will be OK – thankyou for holding the door". She watched him carefully down the three steps and Len lifted his right hand whilst his elbow stayed in his crutch shield and announced "I'm Len and I'm very pleased to meet you! How did you know I was English?" She was too polite to say that she had heard the expletives he had used under his breath whilst trying to negotiate the door and quickly retorted that she had seen the name "Berghaus" on his rucksack.

"I live close to where they are made!" she continued. "My name's Joyce".

Joyce was interested in his condition. In the ensuing discussion Len learned that Joyce's husband was lying seriously ill in hospital. He had suffered a heart attack while they were holidaying in Chamonix. Her situation had so many parallels with Brenda's position ten years earlier. Len knew that the Lord had answered his prayer in the time it had taken him to reach reception from his room on floor five! Here was a woman who could benefit considerably from Brenda's experience, and no one, other than Brenda, was better fitted to counsel her than Len. Joyce obviously appreciated this and before taking her leave of him, for her visit to the hospital, she asked if they could continue their conversation over dinner that evening in the hotel. She also introduced Len to another young woman with whom she had struck up an acquaintance. As Joyce disappeared into the afternoon, Len learned that the newly introduced person was Belgian. She was a courier with a coach party of English tourists and he reasoned that this was God's "quid pro quo". The lady was fluent in English and French languages – and so helpful!

Len explained that he had ambitions to take the cable car up the mountain to the Aguille du Midi, then across the Valley Blanche to the Italian side of the mountain at Helbronner. Instead of looking at him as if he was quite mad in his condition (the reaction he had become good at dealing with) she looked him squarely in the eye and said, "How perfectly wonderful." That caught him off guard. "Just make yourself comfortable, I will go down to the station and check prices and times for you. Don't worry about the weather, the barometer is set fine for a few days!" With this news she was gone!

When she returned, not only did she have the information on the cable car lift, but she also gave him detailed directions to the nearest bank so that he could change his travellers cheques into francs. It took

Len over an hour to get to the bank, no more than a few hundred yards away. He was so tired by the time he reached the counter, his hands were shaking with the amount of energy that he had expended. It was impossible for him to sign the form for release of the French finance. After standing for a few minutes he managed the worst signature he had ever seen and has never understood how the staff were able to equate the spidery scrawl with the original, carefully crafted signature. He was glad that the bank teller had insufficient command of the English language to say, "I feel sorry for you!"

It took most of the afternoon to get down to the bank and back. One moment during the return journey will always remain in Len's memory. He reached a cobbled pedestrian slope, about thirty yards long. The gradient was about 1 in 5. Two small, local urchins had watched him negotiating this for about half an hour with a mixture of amused, (and to Len) unintelligible chatter and looks of concern. Too small to be able to offer physical assistance, they sat on the ground to make themselves more comfortable to witness the complete performance. In the heat of the afternoon, Len was soon bathed in perspiration. The ramp seemed to him to become almost vertical the nearer he got to the top. The forward tilt of the angle of his body became more pronounced with every step and he became acutely aware of the growing excitement of the children. Eventually, he reached the top of the ramp, turned and leaned against a bollard, his own "Mt. Blanc" for the day having been conquered. The youngsters broke into rapturous applause accompanied by loud shouts and smiles of encouragement. "Bravo, Bravo signor" they shouted, obviously thinking anyone so disadvantaged must be Italian! Delighted at their own perspicacity, or genuinely pleased for him, Len will never know, but they ran away down the ramp in a state of high excitement.

What was left of the afternoon and early evening was spent lying on the bed at the hotel, in blissful recovery. From the prone position the ubiquitous summit of Mont Blanc, reflecting the sun, beamed down at him. He would never tire of that view. Later it glowed as if it were on fire as the sun surrendered its life on earth for that day. Len's camera clicked, clicked again, and then God turned out the light and put the mountain to bed for the night.

133

Len looked at his watch....8 p.m.
Time to counsel Joyce in the dining room.

Chapter Twenty-Three –

AGUILLE

"Hello Joyce" said Len as she stood up to greet him to the table, holding out a chair to enable him to sit down. She watched him closely as it took him fully three minutes to turn, throw his crutches to the floor and drop onto the seat.

"I wondered if you would recognise me?" he said.

The remark stopped her in her tracks. She stood back, looked into his flushed face and wondered if he had taken leave of his senses. He shot her his "impish" look, the one he reserves for special friends, the one that he often uses during his talks. A look that told her, to her relief, that she was dealing with a sense of humour, not a crank. The remark "broke the ice", told Len that he was feeling rested and told Joyce that she was in for an entertaining hour. She certainly needed that. Her husband Roger was still seriously ill, although "Showing some sign of improvement," she told Len in response to his question.

Joyce had been in Chamonix for three weeks and the prospect for her was that she would need to stay another month before it would be possible to think of flying her husband home, always, of course, assuming a continuation of his rate of recovery. It did help that he and Brenda had been there before. He regaled Joyce with their story, stressing the significance of the long and vital role played by his wife, and how it had brought him to the point where he dared to have the temerity to embark on an adventure such as he had in mind for tomorrow. Joyce and Robert were similar in outlook to Len and Brenda in that they too had spent much of their leisure life outdoors enjoying mountain walks and adventure. Of consuming interest to Len, they had two sons, both of whom had climbed the Matterhorn!

Even with her present problems, Joyce was certainly not wallowing in self-pity nor lounging about, killing time. It seemed that each morning she had taken an early breakfast, armed herself with a map and walked a scenic mountain route before returning to Chamonix for a visit to her husband at 2 p.m. each day. Len was convinced that the darkest days were past for them. He told Joyce so – just as Ruth Brozy had told him some years earlier. He hoped that, like Ruth, he had been able to put new strength into the hopes of Joyce and Roger.

*   *   *   *   *

The following morning was again fine and the sun winkled Len out of his bed at 7 a.m. He was tempted to lie there with the view of Mont Blanc still intoxicating him, but he had big plans for the day and a Dutch couple, Lardie and Ria Reiters, whom Len had spoken to the previous evening, had promised to consider accompanying him. They eventually decided that they would accompany him to the 'Midi' station and so they solved another major problem for him. It was difficult for Len to understand why he had so many doubts the day previously.

There he was, less than 24 hours later with a string of newly made friends in the hotel, all determined to ensure that he enjoyed his couple of days with them and all seeming to be only too happy to render assistance whenever needed. It was understandable why he had doubts originally. In England the pattern was that wherever he went, people were expecting him because appointments had been made and they were always there to help out when he arrived, if assistance was required. On the continent, he had genuine misgivings because the people were not expecting a paraplegic. One of his facile claims to fame has always been that "When I am sitting, no one would guess that I am paraplegic!" That is certainly true. His legs look perfectly normal when stretched out in front of him, enclosed in perfectly standard trousers, with no weight placed on them. The first time a stranger knows that Len is crippled, is when he stands. From the first second, he needs his crutches to pull himself up and once upright he is heavily dependent upon them. It follows therefore, that when people do not know him, they have to spend some time in Len's company before they appreciate the depth of his disability. When they do, the offers of help flood in. Before going down to breakfast, Len had stood on the balcony thinking he would take a photograph of Dave and Geoff. Pointing the camera for the umpteenth time towards the sparkling white dome, he 'clicked' and said to himself "Well, you're there somewhere. Invisible from this distance, but I wish I could be with you!" There was no time to dwell on it. He had his own plans and they were just about to be put into action. Berghaus on, he went off to the dining room and was determined not to return until he was satisfied that his mission had been accomplished.

The Dutch couple had decided that they would be returning home that day, so any lingering hankering they had to go across the "White World" of Mont Blanc was abandoned to another time but Lardie took Len to the station of the "Midi" and purchased his ticket for him.

They shook hands and said their goodbyes. Lardie heading for Holland, Len to Italy. Odd that Len's biggest headaches were to get to the start point and purchase a ticket. Anyone else would have more problems with rising to a height of almost 13,000-ft in a few minutes and then traversing the Mountain at that consistent height until Italy had been reached. The last two considerations were no problem to Len. He was a child again. Excited to bursting point at the prospect of yet another ambition, which he had nurtured for years, about to happen.

Of his own volition.

It was only 9 a.m., out of school holiday season, yet there were crowds queuing to board the large cable car that transports passengers up to a height of 2,308 metres to Plan d'Aguille, the first stage of the epic journey. He was eyed with a mixture of curiosity, suspicion and, perhaps, sympathy by the milling throng. Suddenly the cable car door was opened and the sympathy all fell apart in a flurry of pushing, shoving, elbows and rucksacks in a display of typical continental courtesy until all were aboard except Len. As he stood contemplating his next move (which would be his first move, so taken aback was he with the speed of the opposition). As if to prove that the age of chivalry had not died completely, a couple of enormous, fair-haired German youths stepped back out of the cabin. They beckoned him to come forward into the place they had occupied, just inside the doorway. So taken was Len with their spontaneous gesture that he thanked them profusely and stepped carefully onto the deck of the cable car. There was just enough room to stand in place of the two of them. Or so he thought! They followed him in immediately and pushed together, so that all other occupants of the cabin found an inch of room each and they were all in, including Len's benefactors. "There's one thing about it." said Len, slightly breathless, "I shall have a job to fall down in this crush!" The level of laughter in the conveyance was such that Len suspected there was a good sprinkling of English bodies in the car. Perhaps, after all, it was *they* who had crampons fixed to their elbows when pushing into the car – not the continentals.

The car came to a halt in minutes and then emptied quicker than it filled up at ground level. It was as if no one had a moment to spare. Len was reminded of the film of the lemmings! Then the need for speed became obvious. The second car that completes the journey to the 'Midi' is much smaller than the first and they were rushing to get to the barrier first to ensure a good place. Len had decided that the whole situation called for a rest to acclimatise before the next stage of the trip, as he half tumbled, half stumbled out of the big car. He more or less fell into the arms of a French attendant, complete with peaked cap and ranks of office on the sleeve, who explained in broken, but perfectly good English, that he would look after him. As he guided Len past the ranks of the opposition, Len decided that perhaps he could finish the journey immediately after all. His attendant was a model of charm and smilingly escorted his charge to the front of the next car as soon as it landed at that junction point. This was to set the pattern for the rest of the day so far as courtesy was concerned and it made Len's holiday, to be treated so generously.

The next part of the climb up the near vertical Aiguille du Midi was awe inspiring as the car almost scraped the rock on the slow, careful last minute or so of the journey upward. The doors opened and there was immediately an icy blast of thin air as the sub-zero temperature, even on a sunny day at Chamonix, greeted the first person out. On this occasion, the populace had the grace to let Len disembark first – and then rush past him yet again to be the first to the next point.

The next stage of the journey to Helbronner on the Italian side of Mont Blanc, involves negotiating a tunnel hewn from the rock of the 'midi'. There is a constant wind through the tunnel at all times of the year and the temperature is more often below zero. Patches of ice on the floor of the tunnel made for a precarious journey. The black eye from the spill on the ferry was still spoiling his delicate facial outline and he was keen to avoid any repeat. Where he could, he negotiated each succeeding placement of his crutches on dry land but he was again operating in a half-light in the tunnel and he was not always sure whether it was dry land or black ice that he was trusting with his life. He progressed with great care.

The traverse of the Valley Blanche is completed in a small cable car seating four people. The cars are grouped together in threes. Tourists often find the height a daunting factor. One starts at 3,842 metres at the Aguille du Midi and is still at a height of 3,466 metres at Helbronner. These heights need a period of acclimatisation and it is not recommended that the trip should form the first venture on any holiday. The temperature is also is a factor to be respected and only with good warm clothing should the trip be undertaken. With a sensible approach however, it is a treat not to be missed, and well within the compass of a reasonably fit person. Len had thought about it a lot. With little in the way of help from his legs and only one lung functioning, it was not something he would want to do every day. But it was worth one supreme effort! As he stood waiting his turn he felt vulnerable. He was slightly breathless. He was experiencing a dull headache, similar to when he climbed his last Italian mountain – the Monte Rosa in 1971. His turn came and he had no time to bewail his fortunes ..... this was what he had come for!

He had been in conversation with a couple from Yorkshire for a few minutes before the cars arrived. With help from an attendant, they hoisted him up the huge step, necessary to negotiate to get into those cabs. Then they jumped into the four-seater and sat opposite Len to enjoy the treat together.

What a treat it turned out to be for them all.

Len sat for a few minutes, beaming across at the couple, Alan and Eileen Lancaster, regained his breath, looked sideways through the window, and immediately was breathless again, this time with the beauty of the utterly spectacular scenery. "My God you've been good to me!" He said the words of thanksgiving out loud, unashamed at his enthusiasm. "Amen!" said Alan and Eileen in unison and they laughed together, exuberant all three at the magic of the world they had found together. It was the first time they had laughed together, but it certainly was not to be the last!

The trip lasts thirty-five minutes one way, and the tiny cable cars are suspended at times, hundreds of feet above the grandeur of some of the most beautiful, accessible, mountain scenery in the world. They were travelling over icefields, glaciers, snowfields, and mountaintops. The Chamonix Needles pointing to the heavens like Cathedral Spires, their forms etched against a cobalt blue sky. Drifting below them crevasses, large enough to swallow a street full of houses. Little black dots on the snow seemed to be moving slowly on zigzag paths – skiers revelling in the late appearance of the summer sunshine. Len stood at the open window of the tiny cab, supported by Alan and Eileen to counteract the movement of the car, slowing at times to a halt, accelerating and then slowing again as he clicked with his camera. He knew from past experience that nothing but the very finest camera could do justice to the views they were experiencing, but he clicked on regardless. Similarly he knew that no words could express the majesty of it all. He wanted time to stand still. He looked at the second hand of his watch. In his 'Alice in Wonderland' world he would not have been surprised if it had stopped. He was disappointed to find it still stuttering mechanically round the dial. What he did know was that he was a child again and it was Christmas morning – no he wasn't a disabled mountaineer getting on in years. He had been left at Chamonix – miles below.

Such a long way from Clent!

Chapter Twenty-Four –

BLUE PETER

At Point Helbronner there is a viewing platform, up several flights of steps. It took him a long time to reach the topmost staging, but he did it! It was 10.15 a.m. and Len, in the company of Alan and Eileen, was glad to be alive, soaking up the sunshine and the rare atmosphere. They had a 360 degree panorama of mountain peaks to study, all appearing to be growing out of a cotton wool base that covered the whole earth – or as far as they could see from their vantage point.

Len spotted what he really wanted to see almost immediately. About fifty miles away he could see the peaks of the Swiss Alps. He identified the Matterhorn, Breithorn, Pollux, Castor, Liskamm and Monte Rosa and for a short while, whilst contemplating the significance they had had on his life, he was quiet. His tongue stilled and his thoughts took over. What memories! No regrets. Just a deep inner sense of immense happiness. He thought of the days when he stood at the top of the Matterhorn.

Alan freely admitted he was no photographer as Len lined himself up with his back to notable landmarks. He had a "Blue Peter" badge in his hat and it was important to him to get a photograph to prove that he had "been there". He had promised Sarah Greene who presented the BBC show at that time that he would let her have just such a photograph. Len's association with her stemmed purely from a daredevil stunt she had performed for the programme when she abseiled from a helicopter. The drop was possibly as high as 200 ft and Len was so impressed that he wrote to her and enclosed a note of his own experience with the helicopter and the effect it had had on his life. She had been so taken with Len's story that she enclosed a "Blue Peter Badge" which was only handed out to "special people". Len did not accept that he had done anything special to deserve it but he guarded it with a jealously protective "feel" for the trophy. The photograph turned out well and was subsequently shown on the programme. The reference to Sarah Greene has a sad, ironic twist, because she and her husband, Mike Smith, were involved in a helicopter accident in Gloucestershire some years later. Sarah lay seriously ill in hospital and Len motored, in his hand-controlled car, to Cheltenham. The hospital receptionist was waiting to greet him and was totally amazed when she saw the badly injured man with crutches negotiating the steps to tap at her window.

"Why didn't you use the hospital facilities and get the porter to wheel you in one of the chairs?" she asked him.

"I don't want any fuss," he informed her confidentially. "Some years ago Sarah sent me a 'Blue Peter' badge. I would like you, in return, to hand her this 'Air Zermatt' badge please."

"Are you telling me that you are not going up to see her after the effort you have made to get all this way?" asked the receptionist.

"No thanks" said Len; "She is entitled to her privacy. I just wanted her to know that her fans haven't forgotten her."

"I know she will be delighted with it," she told Len. "If you knew the tricks that the press reporters have been up to in an effort to see her, you would not believe it! And here I am, offering you a chance to see her and you are turning it down," she smiled.

"The point is," said Len, "some things are more important than invading the private lives of these people when they are both so very poorly. No, I shall be delighted if you can just get it to her for me – I've put a message with it."

Ill though she was at the time, Sarah acknowledged Len's letter from her hospital bed.

That day on the Helbronner trip, dozens of people recognised the Blue Peter badge and remarked to Len that he "must have done something special" to have one of those! He smiled and told them that if they had an hour or so to spare, he would tell them all about it. He was in his element! Joking with the tourists, standing in such grandeur, achieving another of his life's ambitions. He could hardly sit still long enough to have food at lunchtime. He kept getting up and walking around the four sides of the staging viewpoint. Holding on to the sides, looking down the precipitous slopes to the skiers below. Alan managed to disappear for half an hour and came back with face glowing from his exertions in the thin atmosphere to report. "I have been down on the snow Len, standing on the Glacier du Geant. It's absolutely stunning – but I am afraid it's not for you chap! It took me all my time to stand up on the slopes."

Len could not believe that it was 3.15 p.m. and they had been 'on site' for five hours!

It was time to get down to Chamonix again, and then another of those surprise co-incidences occurred. When talking to Alan and Eileen about what they were doing later that evening, Len discovered that they were staying at the same hotel as he. The problem of how to get back to the hotel was no longer. Alan and Eileen were booking out the following morning *en route* for the Bernese Oberland. Joyce would be out on the mountains, walking, before he would be able to get down for breakfast. She had reported a further improvement in her husband's condition, and Len decided at that stage that he would book out in the morning himself, burn his boats and trust to good fortune that he would meet up with the wanderers the following evening back at the camp site.

Before turning in that night, Len looked up again from his balcony at the moonlit white dome, shining in the cold clear air. He saluted his friends, Dave and Geoff, who would be bedding down, up there somewhere. It looked quite impossible that anyone could enjoy a night's sleep in a beautiful but hostile environment like that, but he knew better from his own experience.

"Good night you two! God Bless. Hope you're both still alive. Otherwise how do I get home?" He gave a deep chuckle. He was convinced they could look after themselves. Anyway, he had just asked God to look after them, hadn't he?

Lucky Len! It was the end of another perfect day.

*   *   *   *   *

Friday the 10th September 1982. The friendly faces had gone about their own business. Len had decided he would spend the day at what he called "rest". He took a two-hour walk to cover the half-mile toward the benches at the "midi" station. The noonday sun became too hot for him. He sheltered under umbrellas at a roadside restaurant. He spent the afternoon drinking tea and writing postcards. "Let's see now................. There's the family. Walt Unsworth of 'Climber and Rambler' magazine. (Walt reckoned he had never seen the sun at Chamonix. He must be told that it does visit on occasions). My friends at the British Mountaineering Council. and the Austrian Alpine Club. Sarah Greene of 'Blue Peter'............. Gloria Hunniford, because she had played a record for Brenda, to commemorate ten years since the accident....... The Insul hospital.... Oswestry Orthopaedic Hospital....... and Norman Croucher – now there's a name to conjure with – What a man! The list gets longer – that will account for about 20 cards." Len was speaking quietly to himself as he rummaged through his mind, half-sleeping in the lazy afternoon. What a rare treat!

How can anyone write a card to Norman Croucher and not be moved. Every time Len thought of Norman, he was almost moved to tears because it did not matter what words he was writing, his mind dwelt on the fearsome accident Norman had suffered when crossing a rail line. In seconds this man, as active as Len himself up to the point of his accident, had lost both legs. Whenever he needed inspiration, Len thought of Norman. Since his accident he has performed prodigious feats in getting to the top of mountains, without legs, in the company of giants of the mountaineering scene.

Although he had checked out of the hotel, he made his way back to sit in reception and await the return of his two adventurous friends. There was no sign of them but there were plenty of English people in the hotel to talk to. One couple in particular, a Mr and Mrs Howe, both in their eighties, were glad to sit and chat and to hear the story when they enquired of Len as to how he had met with his disability. "So where are you from?" Len asked them.

"Oh a little village you won't know," they responded with a smile.

"Try me," said Len, "you might be surprised!"

Mrs Howe laughed at the prospect of Len knowing the area. "You won't know it. We live in a tiny village in Norfolk. It's called Old Buckenham"

"Do you know Mr Fellows the head teacher at the High School in Old Buckenham?" Len stunned them both. The elderly couple regarded each other with bewildered looks.

"Are you a joker or clairvoyant?" It was Mrs Howe who first recovered her composure. "I worked with him. I was a teacher myself before retiring!"

Len's face was a picture of triumph. He leaned forward confidentially, his newly bronzed face creased into a knowing smile. "I visited his school last year, and a school in New Buckenham and two schools in er........Attleton....no!..... Attleborough, just down the road from you." He knew more of their ex-teacher friends from the schools he had visited so recently. He had been invited to address Mr Fellows's school with his talk and slides and one invitation had led to another as so often happens. Coincidences like this happen to Len with a regularity which could be called monotonous but for the electrifying effect they always have on him. There is nothing monotonous about that! "It's all part of the rich tapestry," he says.

The Howes made their way from reception to prepare themselves for the evening and Len began to wonder where his friends had got to. By 19.30 hrs he wanted to go looking for them. A man named Mick had just booked into the hotel with his family and he kindly offered to run Len to the campsite at Les Houches, about five miles down the road. The "Claire de Lune" campsite, he recalled, "and the way things are going it will be by the light of the moon before I see them!"

He sat, by the zipped-up tents, having said goodbye to Mick, who obviously had some reservation about leaving him on his own in that position. Len was feeling the hunger pains as he had not eaten since his continental breakfast, twelve hours earlier. He ferreted in the rucksack and found apples, a tomato and a heat affected Kit-Kat bar shaped like a question mark. A three-course meal washed down with a can of warm beer.

The light was fading when he saw two figures that he thought were human, bent double under the weight of their respective ruck-sacks. They were plodding along the road below, still a good few minutes away, single file, separated by the regulation fifteen paces. Len knew it could be no one else. He wanted to jump from his folding chair, shout a greeting to them down below and run along the track to greet them. He felt helpless and suddenly useless. After what he knew would have been a titanic effort on their part for the last two days, he had not prepared a meal for them, had not even "put the kettle on".

They reached their tents, weary and very dirty. "Tell me how did it go? Did you get to the top? How long did it take you to get up? What were the problems? Len was like a child in his excitement. His friends' faces were like marble for a few minutes after they had dropped their sacks to the floor. Underneath the black marks smeared across each countenance was a fresh sunburn that showed up the whiteness of their teeth as smiles lit up their faces. "We dun it," said Geoff in as mock a Black-Country accent as was possible in so few words.

The full story of the two days unfolded as they washed and cooked a meal by torchlight. In their tired condition it took longer than usual and by the time they settled down to savour the gourmet taste that the delay had lent to their meal, the evening was dark, warm and magical under a tranquil blanket of brilliant stars.

The moon rose late that night. Len did not keep them talking for too long.

They had been on Mont Blanc for forty-eight hours.

They had 'bivvied' on the mountain for two nights, preferring to sleep on the mountain rather than use the cramped and dirty huts. Best of all they had journeyed from campsite to summit and back on foot with no recourse to transport. Something they should be rightly proud of. Quiet though they were – he knew they were!

Not only had they achieved one of their burning ambitions, they had also given Len the holiday of a lifetime. Talk about Samaritans? .... Wouldn't it have been easy for them to have turned the other way!

xiv) *Wednesday 28th July 1971 – approaching the Hornli Hutte on the Matterhorn.*

xv) *Len and Alan Plant, on the summit of the Matterhorn. 28th July 1971.*

xvi) *A wooden cross set in stones on the ascent. A moment for contemplation.*

xvii) *Len standing before the North face of the Eiger, July 1972.*

xviii) *Back to the Matterhorn, 23rd July 1972. Roger Massey and part of the team. They agreed to reduce the size of the team to small parties of two and three, to reach the summit.*

xix) *Len's first return to the Alps – 1984.*

xx) 14th July 1990. Len and Brenda, with Lord Hunt, the man who led the first successful expedition to Everest in 1953. This photograph was taken in Zermatt in 1990, on the 125th anniversary of Edward Whymper's first ascent of the Matterhorn.

xxi) *Evening "Cuillins" on the Isle of Skye. One of Len and Brenda's favourite views. The photograph was taken by Robin Wydell in 1999.*

xxii)   *Len's momentous achievement in getting to the top of Kleine Matterhorn is shared with a passing admirer.*

xxiii) *Len with Thomas Aufdenblatten, the man who stayed with him on the mountain through the night of 23rd/24th July 1972.*

xxiv) *Brenda admiring the condition of the helicopter (HB-XDA) that lifted Len from the mountain in 1972. The picture was taken in 1993.*

xxv) *Norman Croucher surprised Len and Brenda in 1993 when he recognised Len's voice in a crowded shopping street in Zermatt. Two climbers with not a useful leg between them.*

xxvi) *Len in chorister's dress at Birmingham Cathedral June 1996. St Hilda's choir sang Evensong. Len has been a member of the choir since he was eight years old.*

xxvii) *On the ascent of the Monte Rosa.*

xxviii) *Thomas and Len, with 'Lucky' Imboden, the first mountain guide to reach Len after his fall.*

xxix) *Resting at 14000 feet 1430 hours.*

xxx) *'Lucky' Imboden, Len and Lucky's brother, Victor. The Imboden brothers found Len, on the Matterhorn in 1972. The occasion was the Centenary of the Mountain Guides Association in 1994.*

xxxi) *A view of the Worcestershire Countryside taken from the four stones on the top of Clent Hills.*

xxxii) *Len with Sir Jimmy Saville MBE at the Robert Jones and Agnes Hunt Spinal Unit, Oswestry. The occasion was the laying of the inaugural stone for the new spinal unit in 1999.* PHOTOGRAPH BY DR CLIVE INMAN

Chapter Twenty-Five –

EACH DAY A BONUS

Back in England again, Len and Brenda settled into the routine of work for her and talks for him. At the same time the garden was becoming more and more reminiscent of an alpine landscape as Brenda, in particular, worked non-stop in her off duty hours to complete the picture. Len "did his bit". He often surprised himself at what he could achieve from his wheelchair. He had been known even to lay paving slabs, but after tipping the chair over a time or two, he decided it was better to lie on the floor and push and pat the paving slabs into position. That way he did not suffer the embarrassment of having to rely on his wife to collect him up so often.

The talks were becoming almost a daily habit. A talk to a group would result in at least one phone call from another group in each area and so he was beginning to find that he would 'appear' in an area several times in a relatively short period, often where he had never set foot before. Clubs, churches, and groups would ask him to go back again year after year when they were preparing their annual diary of events. Len felt that he must vary the delivery and found out old photographs and slides of his holidays in Scotland. He and Brenda had enjoyed them so much, together, before the fall. He visited the air show at Cosford each year and found that he also had sufficient detail to start talking on these visits. The fact that he was now able to vary his talks so much made his services more attractive to the various organisations. How he loved to be able to tell them, when they phoned for his services, that he was now able to offer them a choice of subjects. He often thought back to that first day after his fall. He still marvelled at the skills used by so many people to save this life of his for this special purpose. He was entertaining others with his God given ability to talk. One of his more outrageous dreams was to envisage that he could see them and speak to them. The man and woman who had spent the night on the mountain with him....... the pilot of the helicopter..... the staff at the hospital in Berne..... Ruth Brozy.....

How much he would like to ask them. How much he would like to thank them for what they had done for him. An idle dream, but a warm, recurring theme that helped see him through the good times .... and the not so good times. Len found it difficult to accept that, even occasionally, times were not so good. "Every day is a bonus," he would say, and every morning he woke and thanked God for pointing him in the right direction and showing him the route that Len firmly believed God had mapped out for him.

Len continued to maintain connections with the West Bromwich Mountaineering Club, the British Climbing Club, Halesowen Athletic Club, Tipton Harriers and the thousands of friends he had made through his talks. All kept him abreast of developments and gave him endless opportunities to converse and correspond with interesting people. This is a fact that often surfaces during Len's talks. He will flash a picture onto the screen and point the laser pen to the face of Sir John Hunt (as he then was, later to be Lord Hunt) leader of the first successful Everest Climb in 1953. With pride he glows as he reminds us that it was a British Expedition. With equal pride he points out that the man standing next to Lord Hunt is Len York. Len has pictures of Brenda and himself in conversation with Lord Hunt, pictures of Len walking with Lord Hunt, letters received from Lord Hunt. The crunch line as he addresses the suitably stunned audience is: "How many of you can say you are almost a personal friend of Lord Hunt? How many of you have spoken to him? Do you see what I mean when I say God has directed me along this path? Do you really think that Len York would have been able to get anywhere near Lord Hunt if I had not had my accident on the Matterhorn? Everything happens ..... with a purpose!" The emphasis is on the last three words. Then, whilst his audience is digesting this gem, he flicks the switch to another shot of his beloved Matterhorn and off they go together on another part of a spectacular adventure.

Len has many references to famous people that he could make.

He corresponded in 1983 with Walter Poucher, a man who not only wrote books about mountains but also became the doyen of British Mountain photographers. He was the author of the standard work on cosmetics. He was "a perfectionist, a musician, a doctor of medicine, a chemist, an author, mountaineer, photographer, but above all, a raconteur of tremendous interest." The President of the British Mountaineering Club, Tom Price spoke these words, when presenting Walter Poucher with an engraved glass from Dentdale when the club paid a special tribute to him. Poucher was 90 at the time and had driven himself to the function. Unfortunately his sight failed very soon afterwards but not before he had written Len a beautifully worded letter, some of the points being reproduced now:

"W A Poucher F R P S

Reigate Heath
Surrey
12th June 1983

Dear Mr York,
I was very touched by your letter and enclosures which awaited my
return from the processions of rain I experienced during a five week
visit to the lakes. I had only four sunny mornings when I could work
and must return there in the autumn to try to secure the colour shots
I need for a second book on this very beautiful National Park.
It was a privilege to meet you at the BMC dinner and I much enjoyed
our talk about the mountains we both love.
When I read the details of your fall below the Solvay I marvel at your
recovery and are able today to attain the viewpoints you mention, but
since I am approaching my 92nd year I can no longer climb! and have
to be satisfied with the memories and my camera studies.
Of course, as you must know, my work depends so much on the weather
and taking the photographs that show the most beautiful lines of my
subjects requires a lot of waiting and infinite patience, but the rewards
are immense in the letters and calls I receive from those who just love
the mountains

My second colour book on the HIGHLANDS OF SCOTLAND has just been published and its launching involved numerous appearances on TV and Radio. It will be followed in the autumn by a colour book on the ALPS and I am sure you will appreciate the work that has gone into securing the 100 photographs.
In the meantime I send you my renewed thanks for the pleasure it has given me to meet you at long last.

Yours most sincerely
W A Poucher"

Len keeps with this letter, a spectral landscape, taken by Brenda, in May 1972, with Len in the foreground, and a backdrop of the Cuillin Hills. It was taken from Elgol, only a matter of weeks before the accident. There is a hand-written note which says:

"Excellent shot of the Cuillin from Elgol"   *Signed W A Poucher*

One of Brenda's favourite testaments!

Chapter Twenty-Six –

ALICE AND JACK

It was 1983 and Len's talks were beginning to become an even more important part of his life. Rarely a day went by without the phone ringing and a request for a new venue or a repeat performance at an old venue needing to be arranged.

One such request came from a lady who was president of the Ridgacre Methodist Church, Quinton. A "home" fixture for Len. Mrs Alice Yates was asking him to do a talk for the ladies group at Church. She had heard him talk at a local function and being a keen mountaineer herself, she thought the talk had sufficient to interest her members for an hour or so.

"Be delighted," said Len, "Be delighted to see you all on the 8th." He set the phone onto its cradle and entered the date in his diary. What seemed a routine booking set in train a series of events, which were to have a profound effect on the rest of his life.

The talk was routine. He had enjoyed himself immensely. He had told the ladies that he always got on well with ladies, somehow they felt "safe" with him. "This is possibly because you can run faster than me" he quipped to them from his stance, leaning on his two sticks. "If anyone has any questions I shall be happy to see you whilst we have a cup of tea now."

No one felt safe enough to come forward that afternoon and Alice and Len sat talking together about various points he had mentioned during his talk. He was amazed at the knowledge of this lady, whom he guessed was in her mid-seventies. Any venue he mentioned, whether it was The Lakes, Scotland, Wales: she had been to them all and had a clear perception of many of the spots he considered to be 'secret' to himself. He went on to talk of the Alps, and still she was with him all the way. She spoke with him about Zermatt and stunned him by saying that she had visited the Matterhorn in 1965, on the Centenary celebration of the first climb by Whymper and his party. She had even climbed as far as the Hornli Hut, a five-hour test for any mountaineer. When she had arrived at the hut, Alice and her husband Jack had been disappointed that they could go no further because the BBC and Swiss TV had commandeered the Matterhorn from that point on and had erected platforms for the filming they were doing. The celebration of the first climb was big business to them and too good an opportunity to miss. Len knew then that he was talking to a serious mountaineer. He enquired as to where her husband was, and she said he would have been with her at the talk that day but for the fact that it was a 'ladies only' event. "I'm only glad the exclusion of males did not apply to the speaker," said Len and they both enjoyed the joke.

Alice and her husband had climbed the Wildspitze, Ortler, Monck, Marmalada and Zugsplitze as recently as 1982. They were extremely active and "hopeful of managing one or two more," as she put it.

That night, Alice went home and told Jack all about this "young" man of fifty-six and the story he told. She enthused about the spiritual and entertaining way he had of delivering the tale. How remarkable she thought he was, to be taking his heavy disability in such a constructive and philosophical manner. "What an inspiration" she said. They talked about Len well into the night.

Whether it was because of the talk they were not sure, but they decided their very next holiday would be spent in Zermatt. They had not visited the resort since 1965 and it would be good to see how the place had changed. Anyway, the place was surrounded by the type of mountains they appreciated and, given good weather, they could not help but enjoy the experience again.

When they last visited Zermatt they had travelled under the umbrella arrangements of the "Holiday Fellowship" but this time they made their own way by air and then rail. As the train moved along the valley towards it's final stop Alice tugged at Jack's sleeve and said, just a mite wistfully, "It would be nice if we could make contact with the man who stayed on the mountain that night and rescued Len York, don't you think?" Jack chuckled at the audacity; "Do you really think there's any chance o' that? After all these years?"

Cars are not allowed in Zermatt, so they disembarked at the station and looked at the attractive walk up the main street towards the mountain that dominates the whole scene. Carrying heavy rucksacks on their backs they walked for a few minutes and were taken aback at the amount of development that had mushroomed since their last visit. When they thought about it, it had been almost twenty years since they last set foot in the village and it perhaps was not so surprising that the scene had changed fairly radically. It was the number of hotels, in particular, that seemed to have increased beyond all recognition. The main street was lined with fairly expensive-looking accommodation and as the rate of exchange of the pound versus the Swiss franc was not particularly favourable, they thought somewhere more modest would suit them. Not cheap mind, but then nothing was cheap in Switzerland, but nothing was quite like it, and they could afford something in the 'three star' ratings they thought.

Meandering to the left at the top of the main street they looked at a couple of boards advertising meals. If they turned around to look along the pathway (it was too narrow to be a road) they caught the view of the mighty Matterhorn, framed between two hotel blocks and it seemed to be leaning towards them in a beckoning movement from the top third of it's bulk. Turning again to resume their walk they thought the newish building to the left, in front of them, looked inviting. It seemed to be hiding behind some low trees but it had a friendliness exuding from it somehow and they decided this would be the hotel that they would try first. They supposed that if they spent a couple of nights there, they could always move on if they were not satisfied.

The Alpina Hotel was better than they dared hope. It was not expensive by Swiss standards. It was clean and the atmosphere was friendly from the first contact. As expected, the owners spoke good English and they welcomed walkers. What more could they hope for? The couple settled themselves in for what they could sense was going to be a holiday with a special meaning for them both. They had planned to spend the whole two weeks in Zermatt and after the first seven days they were relaxed and delighted by the weather. Close by, they had accessibility to transportation that would help them to the top of numerous mountains. They were beginning to get a good deep tan and their exposure to the wine-like Swiss air had given them good breathing and made them feel fit to tackle anything Zermatt had on offer – apart, that is, from the Matterhorn itself. They reasoned that it was an expensive undertaking to have a guide to help them and it was a journey that, at their age, they would not want to undertake themselves without a guide.

It was at the start of the second week. Alice told Jack that she felt she really had to do something about trying to find out what she could about Len and if anyone remembered the rescue. "I think I will go over to the guide office and see if anyone there can tell me, or point me in the right direction at least," she said to Jack.

"Well I don't know about you!" Jack cautioned. "You really have got a bee in your bonnet about this chap Len York. You've got to be wasting your time after so long but I suppose you'd better go if it will satisfy you. I'll clean the boots for tomorrow while you're gone!" He moved out onto the balcony as Alice pulled the bedroom door shut. Jack took his field knife and started scraping at the stubborn mud that clung to the outside of the sole of his boot and stabbed at the dried deposits between the treads. He thought how well the boots were standing up to the many mountains they had climbed over the years and congratulated himself on what a good buy they had been when he picked them up in a sale in the Peak District so many years before.

At ground level, nowhere is very far from anywhere else in Zermatt, and it was not long before he heard Alice tapping at the room door. "Well, that didn't take you long" he said, taking a step back to give her space to walk past, "I can tell by your face you haven't had any luck," he continued sympathetically, "What did they say?" She brushed past him as he pushed the door closed.

"They weren't terribly helpful." she responded as she settled herself carefully on the bottom edge of one of the twin beds that took up much of the space in their comfortable room. "The guide said, 'We have many, many of them every year. Some die, some live'. I am beginning to think it will be impossible. He asked me how long ago it happened and when I told him twelve years he was too polite to laugh, but made it clear with a spread of the hands that there was no hope."

"Don't get too dejected about it dear. We are having a lovely holiday, and Len wouldn't want you to spoil it now, would he?" Jack reasoned.

"I suppose you are right you old know-all!" she responded, and her faced creased into her old familiar beaming smile. Jack knew from that moment that nothing was about to sour what was turning out to be a memorable holiday among the many memorable holidays they had shared.

Later that evening, in the dining room, Jack watched as Alice finished off the remains of the apple strudel that he had passed to her. It was unusual for him, he was normally very partial to this particular sweet and no one does it better than the Swiss. For some reason he didn't feel too hungry that night but Alice obviously appreciated it as she cleared her plate.

Elizabeth, the lady of the house, with typical Swiss thoroughness, made it her business to ensure that her guests were happy with the accommodation in general and the meal in particular. They were not disappointed that evening.

"Good Evening," she said, and then continued in her flawless English, her face radiating her warm personality, "And what have we been doing today?" This was a sign that, after a week's acquaintance, she need not ask if they had enjoyed their food or if they had had enough of it. She knew by then that her guests would let her know if the service was lacking or the standard had slipped. It was an acceptance of them as friends; that she was genuinely interested in their walks and climbs and she had an admiration for the way they coped with the stiff tests provided by the local features.

"We have been up to Rifflealp," Jack ventured "Do you know it?" he teased, knowing that she had spent most of her life in the area. Elizabeth burst into involuntary laughter, immediately spotting his scarcely veiled attempt at humour.

"It is my favourite place" she exclaimed. "It is where you take the very best pictures of the Matterhorn," she said in a matter of fact tone. "Did you eat at Freddies place? The views from there are wonderful!"

"Yes," they had eaten at Freddie's place and "Yes," they too thought the views were wonderful.

"Did you go anywhere else?" she asked.

"No, we were tired when we finished walking down from the Rifflealp and thought we would call it a day!" said Alice. "How do you mean, call it a day?" asked Elizabeth, and they smiled together at Jack's explanation of the English colloquialism.

"No, we did nothing else apart from Alice going over to the guide shop." Jack was teasing Alice now and he waited for a reaction but Elizabeth beat her to it.

"Why did you go over to the guide shop Alice? Do you want to go up the Matterhorn?" It was Elizabeth's turn to tease.

Alice explained about Len and Elizabeth listened attentively, they agreed twelve years ago would stretch anyone's memory. "I know," said Elizabeth, "In that time there are so many incidents on the mountain and many end tragically. Some years ago my husband was a guide and he was called out sometimes several times a week. Ah – there's chef waving to me - it must be time for the staff to sit down to our meal. I will wish you goodnight then – unless you are coming to the bar for a drink tonight?"

Alice and Jack excused themselves for that evening – they were both tired and they opted for a full night's sleep.

Chapter Twenty-Seven –

REVELATION

The Yates were early down to breakfast the following morning. It was their intention to go up to Klein Matterhorn and then walk back from the intermediate stage. Looking through the dining room window the prospects for a good day were improving with every minute. The early morning mist and slight drizzle were clearing before the effects of the warming sun and they felt it in their bones that this was to be a big day. They could hardly wait to get started.

Just as they were clearing the last dregs of coffee from the pot on the table, Elizabeth appeared from the kitchen end. This was unusual at breakfast time. She was normally too busy in the kitchen to be able to put in an appearance, but that day she stood waving a piece of paper in her hand smiling broadly down the full length of the room. As soon as eye contact was established she started to walk quickly towards them, still waving the paper in her hand.

Jack and Alice were baffled, did she have a letter for them ..... or a telegram perhaps? Whatever, it did not look like bad news as she approached them waving the paper and chattering to them. It sounded like, "I've found it – I'm sure I've found it. This is it – look – is your friend's name Charles Leonard York?" The couple looked at each other and then back to Elizabeth, they were still not quite sure what she was saying. Elizabeth put the letter on the table so that they could see it. This caused Alice immediately to ferret in her handbag for her spectacles, as it was clearly an important document – if it referred to Len. The spectacles did not help – the letter was not written in a language decipherable to her, but Elizabeth persisted. "It is from Marie Louise to Thomas, it was written twelve years ago and it is all about the rescue that she and my husband were involved in. It says the man who was rescued was Charles Leonard York."

"It was my husband who rescued him!"

For a second Jack and Alice looked at each other in disbelief and then the significance of it all dawned on them simultaneously. Not only had they discovered the identity of the man and woman involved in the rescue of their friend Len but they were here, alive, approachable, friendly and with a written record that Elizabeth had filed away twelve years before. A testament to her filing system! A testament to Alice's obsessive sense of purpose.

The bee had been dramatically released from her bonnet!

Jack tried to restrain Alice – she chattered incessantly. He had rarely seen her so excited. She chatted on about all sorts of things for about ten minutes and finally announced that she felt like going home there and then to break this news to Len. Firmly but gently, he talked her round. It wasn't normal for her to be impractical.

Chapter Twenty-Eight –

THE LETTER

Len paused for a second to admire again the classic outline of the Cuillins on the print that he was putting into a plastic sleeve. The photograph was bound for his detailed scrapbook that gave him so much pleasure. Records he and Brenda had maintained since their cycling days. He found the stiffness of his fingers and the slippery surface of the sleeve to be an irksome duet but he knew the therapy was worth the odd mild curse. That particular morning he was relaxed. He had no meetings that day so he decided to catch up on the administration that had got way behind over the past few weeks. He wasn't aware of the news that was about to break, and his actions for the rest of the day would be dictated by a change of plan. He heard the "splat" of the letters as they dropped to the floor in the hall. Irene, their popular, good-humoured post-lady, walked away down the drive, another busy day in front of her.

Swinging himself up onto his sticks, Len made progress slowly to the door, cocked one stick under his left arm, bent carefully to the floor and picked up two letters. One was from the Midlands Electricity Board and immediately placed to one side, unopened, on the hall table. The other one looked more interesting. It was hand-written and posted locally. He held it, slightly crumpled, in his right hand, against the crossbar of his stick, as he made his way back to the table in the lounge. He hummed the "toreador" song from "Carmen" with his tongue against the top of his palate. He sang in time to his progress along the hallway – a somewhat slower tempo than that of the stage performance.

He meticulously placed his well-used paper knife between the envelope and it's flap and eased the two apart. It bore an address in Quinton – not more than two miles away and said:

21.6.84

"Dear Len
You may be able to remember us – we attend Ridgacre Methodist
and have seen your 'Matterhorn' lecture twice. Jack was able
to supply you with a transparency of the 1965 helicopter!
Well, we have just returned home after two weeks at Zermatt.
We stayed at the "Alpina" Hotel, which is run by a young couple,
the Aufdenblattens. The husband has been a guide and we discovered
he was the young man who helped you when you had the accident.
He was on duty that night at the Hornli hut, along with a young
nurse – Marie-Louise. The Aufdenblattens showed us the letter written
to them by a lady in Berne, to whom you had sent a letter of thanks.
This lady sent a translation to the Aufdenblattens. They treasure this
and were thrilled to hear how you have progressed.
I was going to send them an article that had been published by the
'Mail' about two years ago, but I just cannot find it. Have you any
recent pictures of yourself, or article you could let us have to forward
to them?
Thomas signed the enclosed card for you – and when you are in Zermatt
again, they would love to see you.
The hotel is near the church, in the centre of Zermatt.
We found Zermatt changed! – more crowded, and more hotels.
We were last there in '65. We started off with snow, but after
three days we had brilliant sun. Spring had a slow start, but the
flowers were showing – the trees put on leaves, and it was full
summer in a week!
The snow was low, and walking tracks not clear, but we were
out every day. The mountain stood out proudly most days.
With our warm greetings.
Jack and Alice Yates"

The beautifully simple letter would normally have bought a quiver to his bottom lip but that day he was caught unawares. He wasn't expecting it and the message it contained stunned him on first reading. The rendition of "Toreador" had stopped long since. He read it again in silence and the magnitude of what this gentle, elderly couple had achieved, with no prompt from him, other than a fleeting reference in his talk at some time, caused him to catch his breath. He had not had time to appreciate that those few lines would change the whole course of his future and had added a new dimension to his story. What he did appreciate immediately was that this was a further miraculous twist in the 'miracle' of his life since the accident.

The lip quivered; his face crumpled; a child again, before forces in which he believed, but did not quite understand.

Len wept.

Chapter Twenty-Nine –

ALPINA

Things began to happen quickly after the letter from Alice and Jack Yates. Len phoned them of course, as soon as he had recovered his normal good-natured equilibrium.

"God moves in a mysterious way his wonders to perform" was Len's opening remark.

Alice recognised his voice immediately and responded, as Len had expected, "He plants his footsteps in the sea and rides upon the storm." The words of a well loved hymn written by William Cowper two hundred years before.

Alice and Jack were thrilled at Len's reaction to their news. "If it were Christmas, and I was five years old I could not be more delighted" he said. "I see this as a wonderful adjunct to the story – I shall now be able to fill in the part of the story that I have not been able to tell with complete accuracy – what happened during the night on the mountain." His mind was already working on the permutations and possibilities of how he may pursue this new information. His first task was to get in touch with the guide; a man he now knew was named Thomas Aufdenblatten. Alice had told him how pleasant and approachable a young man Thomas was. He and Elizabeth had taken over the business when it became too much for Thomas's parents. They seemed to be running a thriving business and she was sure he would receive a warm welcome from them if he decided to contact them.

"If?" said Len, "If? Just lead me to them. I can't wait, I don't know whether to phone, write or fly over to see them unannounced. I just can't wait! I hope I shall settle down over the next few days and become more rational about it all, but for the present I am higher than the Matterhorn about this."

He did settle. Within a few days Len had written to Thomas and Elizabeth and they responded almost immediately. Whilst letters were being exchanged he had contacted his friend David Munslow who had immediately agreed to go again with him to Zermatt, "As soon as you like" was his response and plans were made for them to visit Zermatt and stay at the "Alpina" hotel in August 1984.

The trip was extended into a twelve day holiday and five days were again spent under the north face of the Eiger on a camping field but for once the biggest thrill of a holiday for Len was not the mountains but the meeting with his hosts.

On the 20th September 1984 the three of them, Elizabeth, Thomas and Len were photographed together for the first of many times. On that occasion, Len had forsaken his sticks and propped himself up with one arm around the shoulders of Elizabeth and one arm around the shoulders of Thomas. This couple had unknowingly formed a "prop" for him from the very night of his accident, something over twelve years earlier. Elizabeth for having the foresight to have her nurse friend Marie-Louise staying with them and Thomas for the considerable part he played in the rescue.

"I know I have a reputation for being something of a talker," said Len, "But no words of mine could convey the joy of that re-union."

The friendship between Len, Brenda and the Aufdenblattens blossomed. After the first visit to the Hotel 'Alpina' in 1984 Len was to make it a pilgrimage each year. In 1988 Brenda accompanied him and was introduced for the first time to Elizabeth and Thomas. It was a particularly memorable visit because their hosts made quite a party of it for them and Len considers now that each time he and Brenda undertake the trip the whole period is a 'party'.

Thomas obviously considers it to be an occasion for his family. "We do not have to book any entertainment for the hotel," he says, "when Len is here for the fortnight he entertains all my guests for me! Most nights the guests can't wait to congregate in the lounge of the hotel and enjoy the fraternity that Len's presence always seems to generate."

On that first trip for them both in 1988 the abiding memory was when Len and Brenda boarded a helicopter in Zermatt to be taken round the summit of the Matterhorn. The pilot was aware of Len's story and made the very most of the flight for them. He circled the mountain no less than five times, altering the focus from the top to the bottom of the mountain in stages so that Len could explain to Brenda what it was like to stand on the top of the mountain. He was able to point out the route down the snow shoulder and where the Solvay hut was in relation to the top. He showed her the Hornli hut and the spot between the two huts where the accident happened. An exhilarating experience for anyone, but for Len it was again, the trip of a lifetime. For him it provided a feeling of utter pleasure and contentment that comes with the fulfilment of another powerful ambition. The ambition he had to show Brenda what it was that drove him to make the climb and the sense of achievement that flows from the successful culmination of that climb – certainly on the first occasion. His face, and hers, radiated their pleasure at the end of a flight that they will always remember. Len has been heard to say that it looks far more difficult from the aircraft than it does on the mountain. "If I had done the helicopter flight first, I would not have climbed it," he quips at any opportunity.

The thrill of the flights around the mountain was eclipsed only by a further discovery that was made after the helicopter landed on the pad.

It was the same helicopter! The same craft that had lifted him from the mountain sixteen years before!

It bore the number – HB XDA.

It looked immaculate and so far as Brenda and Len were concerned it would have passed off as a new one, so well do the crew and ground staff maintain the machine.

The 1989 visit to Zermatt was notable for the number of people they met in casual conversation who turned out to be 'connected', or in some way, to have links with them. The first was when travelling from Zurich by train to Brig. Len, as usual, had to explain to the couple across the gangway, how he came by his injury. The fellow interrupted him at the mention of the 'Alpina' Hotel.

"Just a minute" he said, "You stayed at the 'Alpina' last year? So did we! Thomas told us all about you both. It's Len and Brenda isn't it?

Well what a co-incidence!" They introduced themselves as David and Eileen Irvine from Manchester and the four-hour journey from Zurich to Brig flew by in what seemed a few minutes. At one stage Len was bold enough to make a comment about David's rather classy-looking white sports shoes.

"Yes," came the reply, "They were given to me at Wimbledon by Boris Becker."

Len was in full flight by this time and felt he knew the man well enough to say, "Now look, I have lost the use of my legs but I haven't lost my senses – not yet. You're pulling my leg! I can't feel which one it is - but you are, aren't you?"

But he wasn't. David turned out to be the sports correspondent of the "Guardian" newspaper and Boris Becker had given the shoes to him – presumably because a week or so before, Boris had won the Wimbledon championship. David then proceeded to enthral Brenda and Len with a succession of tennis stories – incidents that had occurred all over the world. Unusually for Len, he became the listener – and how rich were the stories that came over to Brenda and him from the other side of the carriage.

Their luck held – on the short journey from Brig to Zermatt they met Ken and Janet Marshall. No prizes for guessing which hotel they had booked into in Zermatt – yes the 'Alpina' again. How well connected were the Aufdenblattens! Ken was a well-known mountain marathon man. He had completed four, one hundred-mile mountain cross-country runs and was well known to Len through his own running connections. He was to prove a boon to Len, and Brenda, as he took over much of the pushing of the wheelchair for the next ten days. Some journeys were accomplished at break-neck speed with the enthusiasm of Ken. "Break-neck" speed providing a focus of humour for both Len and Ken, a point they returned to time and again in the re-telling of their adventures.

Brenda and Len took the wheelchair to one of their favourite spots – the Rifflealp. It proved to be a boon for the journey from the station to "Freddie's" restaurant. Freddie asked Len to sign the visitors book and he was moved to find that it was obviously an honour to be asked to pen something within it's pages. The entries looked like a litany of the "Hall of Fame". Len joked with Freddie when he came across an entry from Paul McCartney about two pages back from where his own entry would appear. "I'll bet money that when he made that entry, Paul never expected anyone so famous as Len York would be putting his name in the book!"

That evening, when they returned to the hotel, they were greeted at reception by Elizabeth's voice. It almost sang to them. "Ah, Brenda and Len there's a lady waiting to see you." They were trying to disentangle Len from the wheelchair so that he could make his way up the few steps to the first landing level. He was over-tired following the day out and really was not in any condition to entertain anyone, but Elizabeth's voice was compelling. He knew he had to turn around to see who this person would be. He really was put about as there were several people in the reception area forming an audience. It was unlike Len to be unprepared for an audience. He turned, and in front of him stood a slim, attractive young woman with a smile as welcoming as the rising sun. Len was a picture of self-consciousness as he fumbled for the right words. He did not know her and as he hung on his crutches supporting his weary body, he struggled out the words. "Well, I don't know you, but is it? ...can it be.....Marie Louise?" The way her smile burst into a cry of delight told him she *was* Marie Louise. They embraced warmly, with their arms around each other, almost bringing his frail form to the ground. For the second time in his life, Marie-Louise was supporting this lucky man!

Another perfect day had produced another magic moment for Len and Brenda to share.

They were to meet Marie-Louise's son Tony, who was twelve years old. He visited Brenda and Len's room before the evening meal. Cradled carefully in his arms he held a present. It was a photograph of the Alps that Tony, his mother Marie-Louise and their family could see from their house, at Gochenen. It was blown up to a size three feet long by eighteen inches deep and now hangs prominently in the York's home at Halesowen.

That night there was much talk between them. Mostly it was of the eventful seventeen years since they had spent the night on the mountain together. While they chatted, the Matterhorn smiled down on them. A silent witness..... the summit bathed in moonlight...... the benign tiger........for that night!

*   *   *   *   *

The following day Brenda and Len were able to meet Marie-Louise's husband – Moses. With him, were their two younger children, daughter Olivia and the baby, Mattreis. Marie-Louise had pushed the wheelchair to a local park where they were able to pose for photographs together.

Moses is a mountain guide and their son Tony, mountain-crazy. A climber at twelve years of age, he went away clutching a West Bromwich Mountaineering Club sweatshirt, a present from Len and Brenda.

"Not many of those in Gochenen I'll be bound!" said Len as he presented it to the delighted youngster.

Chapter Thirty –

ANNIVERSARY

Almost twelve months later saw Brenda and Len in Zermatt again, for the celebration of the 125th anniversary of the successful but tragic, first climb of the Matterhorn, by Edward Whymper and his party. As Brenda pushed him, in his wheelchair, up the main street, on their journey from the rail station, Len was excited by the atmosphere of Carnival.

Brenda concentrated solely on propelling the heavy chair and occupant safely towards the 'Alpina', but he was captivated. Buildings festooned with bunting. Flags and banners suspended across the street and draped from each storey of every building. A riot of tangled colour provided by the cascading flowers that dripped from each crowded window box. The whole scene surmounted by the magnificence of the beckoning peak standing sentinel. It came into overpowering view, majestic as ever, as they turned sharply left, by the side of the Roman Catholic Church, at the top of the main street. Brenda paused for a moment to take a breather and have her first glimpse of the magic peak for that year. She walked in front of the chair to enquire and tease him, "So what is so special about today then?"

He had anticipated her, his broadest smile displayed for the occasion, his head looked from the sun-drenched East face on the right to the 'Alpina', slightly downhill now and to his left. He brought his head round again to face his wife and, in a half whisper from his heavily creased smile he breathed "This is the stuff of life!"

Brenda knew it was no good trying to talk him out of his ecstatic reverie. He was the "happiest man in the world." He told everyone he met so. There were times when she had her private doubts, but she knew, certainly at that moment; *he was.* It was tough work for them both to get to Zermatt each year, but he was never happier than when he was there; and she was beginning to get the same feeling. The place was beginning to mean almost as much to her as it always had done to Len. Whether it was because of the number of people who waved a genuine welcome to them as they walked up the street. Whether it was the warmth of the greeting she knew Elizabeth and Thomas would show to them and sustain for the next two weeks. Or whether she was just falling in love with the beauty of this part of the world, she was not quite sure. Just like Len, she felt a refreshing 'tingle' each time she came to Zermatt. She knew 'nice' things were going to happen to them in the next two weeks, and she wasn't to be disappointed.

The very next morning Len sat at one of his favourite spots, in what seemed to him to be the eternal summer that blesses Zermatt for their holidays. He was back in the square in front of the Roman Catholic Church where he had felt so close to peace the day before. Brenda had taken the opportunity to spend a few minutes in the shops. They always held a magnetism for her. A hundred yards or so from where he sat, Len saw Thomas deep in conversation with a thickset, powerfully built young man. They walked slowly together and suddenly quickened pace when Thomas spotted Len looking towards them. "Good Morning Len," he shouted across the square raising his right arm in international recognition. The two of them quickened their pace and stopped a couple of yards from him. "We were just talking about you." said Thomas, "I was reminding my friend here who you are. I would like you to meet a very good friend of mine....... Len....... this is Lucky Imboden!

Thomas did not have to say any more. Len still felt the urge to get up quickly from his seat on just such an occasion. He wanted to shake the hand of the man who had first made his way up the mountain to report his position on the night of his accident. He did not need to move from the seat. Lucky was obviously mutually pleased to meet this 'phenomenon' named Len York. His handsome, smiling face sported an enormous military style handlebar moustache that moved in an exaggerated way when he laughed or when he spoke. He leaned towards the chair and shook Len's hand with a special warmth. A moving moment for each of them. He had been well primed by Thomas and all three spent an hour talking over their joint experience.

The actual day of the anniversary started for Len at 4.30 a.m. It was at this time that the Swiss TV service put on a broadcast of a live 'climb' of the Matterhorn by way of tribute to Whymper's party. Len made his way, on his crutches, in the darkened hotel, to the TV lounge. He was in splendid isolation. He had reminded everyone in the hotel about the programme before they had retired the previous evening but it looked as if he alone had the impetus to make the effort at so early an hour. And so it was..... but only for fifteen minutes. While he watched the screen, the fingers of his hands gripped the arms of his chair. He was in rapt attention. Anticipating a six-hour vigil, he followed the string of climbers, identified only by the lights of their helmet lamps – in complete darkness. They threaded their way, in file, along a ridge to the vertical neck wall that signals the start of the climb. At that moment – at that unearthly hour – he was aware of a form making herself comfortable beside him. It was 4.45 a.m. and he knew immediately who it was who had the courage and the enthusiasm to keep him company.

"Brenda - bless you!" he said, quietly into the darkness. "Now that has really made my day – (or night?)."

They held hands. Suddenly it was 1952 and they were on the back row at the Warley Odeon again.

*   *   *   *   *

"Now perhaps you will believe me," he whispered, squeezing her hand, "you really do have to start in the very early, cold morning darkness and in the most inhospitable conditions."

"Oh I always believed you Len," she said, "I always believed you! What were you starting on?"

The only thing he could see in the darkness was the flashing glint of her knowing eyes, reflected from the light of the screen. They stifled their merriment in hand protected sniggers .... or they would wake the whole of the sleeping hotel.

Len watched, riveted, as the climbers reached the point where the whole body cries out in protest in the thin air at 10,600 feet. The exertion, the slipping and sliding, the thought of unknown perils that lie ahead. Yet he would willingly change places now with any one of them, right there and then. Instead of thinking of the 1972 fall, his mind unconsciously switched to the much sweeter memory of 1971, when he and four other members of the West Bromwich Mountaineering Club set out at the same time, in similar circumstances, to stand on the top of the mountain at 8.30 a.m. and had a wonderful day. One of the unforgettable thrills on that day was to see the very tip of the east face of the Matterhorn, bathed in the reflected golden glow of the rising sun, whilst all the mountains around were still lost in darkness. He saw the spectacle again, from the settee in the lounge of the 'Alpina', on the TV screen. If he could make his way fifty yards up the slope from where they sat, he would see it again, "in the raw", but he chose not to. He would lose the effect that was calling to him from the TV picture. A black cloak was being slowly drawn down the face of the mountain. Slowly, it revealed to the cold of the morning, the unique outline of one of God's most compelling creations.

By 6 a.m. Len could sit no longer and he was lured into the street to take a photograph of the scene that was now lit fully by the sun. He returned to the TV screen to witness the familiar sights of the Solvay hut and the snow shoulder at 14,000 feet and later the cameras caught to perfection the elation of the climbers as they reached the summit. There was plenty of help for the TV cameramen from the local helicopter crews and Len was so drained that he felt as if he had climbed the mountain again. He recovered sufficiently to muster the energy to devour the breakfast bought to him on a tray, at about 8 a.m., by Elizabeth.

Later that same day, Brenda and Len made up part of the congregation for a service in St Peter's, the church of the Alpine Club. The church was built by the British in 1870 and provided a considerable test for Len to climb the steep double bank of steps by which the building is fronted. The service was to commemorate the first successful climb of the Matterhorn one hundred and twenty-five years earlier and was conducted by the Bishop of Dunwich, the Rt. Rev E N Devenport. Lord Hunt (At that time Sir John Hunt) was in the crowded congregation, as were other members of the Alpine Club. After the service Lord Hunt spoke with Brenda and Len and spent some time recalling their previous meeting four years earlier at the British Mountaineering Club dinner.

The following day a church service was held in the open-air at the Catholic Church. Again it was well attended, several hundred people taking advantage of the good weather. The choirs sang, the bands played and a bronze statue of Edward Whymper was consecrated. These activities were followed by a procession in folk costume, all played out beneath the omnipresence of the mountain. Brenda took a memorable photograph of the Bishop of Dunwich and Lord Hunt in procession with other members of the Alpine Club. The two principal protagonists were glad to receive a copy of the photograph, as they had not had an opportunity to take a record for themselves. These happenings formed the focus of their visit to Zermatt in 1990 and their friendship with Angela and Michael Clarke began. For Angela, the friendship was to prove tragically short-lived. She died of cancer very soon after their meeting, but the bond with Michael has blossomed strongly in the years since.

Brenda and Len went again to Zermatt in 1991 and 1992, renewing their many friendships and building others. 1991 was noted for the fact that an entrance gate and wheelchair ramp was put in at the entrance to St Peter's Church, a boon to Len, who had led something of a campaign about this since 1988.

1992 was the year when Brenda, in borrowed boots, reached the Hornli Hut with six other people. This was by far the most difficult test she had undertaken in twenty years. Len had waited for five and half-hours for her to return to the cable car at Schwarzsee. When she finally returned he listened to her story with unconcealed enthusiasm as she related the day's happenings. The adventure had culminated in Brenda climbing for a short way, up the first slab. The climb they had watched together, on TV, in the darkness of early morning, two years earlier.

They also circumnavigated the Matterhorn again, in the helicopter, flying within fifty feet of the face. They had a wonderful view of a climb in progress involving three climbers on the knife-edge ridge above the snow shoulder at 14,000 feet. They also had a close-up view of the summit cross at 14,787 feet.

In July 1993 they were in Zermatt again. Len in his favourite spot, taking the sun, in the square outside the Roman Catholic Church. He is convinced that, as is said about Piccadilly Circus, if one spends enough time there, the whole world passes by – certainly the climbing world seems to. Apart from the famous, he meets friends and lots of people from home who have been in the audience at his talks. They are all on holiday and they all have time to spend a few minutes chatting. How Len responds to that environment! Thomas is right when he says that "Everyone knows Len in Zermatt!" and we know how much Thomas and Elizabeth look forward to the annual visit of Brenda and Len. On that July afternoon in 1993, Brenda had rejoined Len in the square and they were looking in the window of one of the many fascinating shops.

A voice from behind them said, "You two are a long way from home!" They each turned their head to be greeted by the smiling face of a tall well-built man – dark haired, with a black, short cropped beard and moustache. He carried a heavy rucksack on his back with full camping gear.

"Norman Croucher!" Len exploded, at the unexpected pleasure. "What a wonderful surprise. How long are you here for? Where are you staying? What are you doing these days?" The questions tumbled from Len at this bolt from the blue. It was five years since they last met and Norman, walking past the shop, had recognised Len's voice, before he had caught sight of him.

Another excuse to sit for an hour and swop stories. Len reminded Norman of their meetings. They had met in 1982 at the Annual General Meeting of the Alpine Club at Ambleside in the Lake District, and in 1983 at the AGM of the UK Branch of the Austrian Alpine Club at Llanberis. The last occasion when Norman addressed a meeting was at Birmingham University in March 1988. To Len, this was a man who was the epitome of courage. Having lost both legs in a horrific accident when a train ran over them, he found the most difficult part of his recovery was coming to terms with the fact that he himself had caused the accident which deprived him of his limbs. He admits that he had been drinking when the accident happened. He had slipped down a railway embankment and the train had run over his legs, severing them below the knees.

Six months after the accident he was fitted with artificial legs and almost immediately he started training. After some exercise scrambling and then pulling himself up cliffs with his arms, Norman set about the nine hundred miles walk from Land's End to John O' Groats. He admits it was really a stern test for him, but it soon hardened up his soft limbs. This is how he prepared the way for his exploits in conquering some of the most difficult mountain climbs in the world, often in the company of some of the biggest names in world mountain climbing. He had been awarded the OBE, had twice been voted "Man of the Year" and won an international award for "Valour in Sport".

In qualifying for the awards, in the Alps, he had climbed the Matterhorn, the Eiger and Mont Blanc. He had climbed on some of the highest peaks in Bolivia and went to Africa with Chris Bonington.

Standing in the square together in Zermatt, Len on his sticks, Norman in moleskin trousers and trainers – with not a good leg between them. It is unlikely that anyone not knowing them would have guessed. One thing is certain. No one in the world would have been happier than the pair of them while they exchanged details of their latest exploits.

Just to make sure they didn't have it all their own way, Brenda capped it again by producing a stunning photograph of them.

Chapter Thirty-One –

HER MAJESTY'S PLEASURE

One of the great joys for Len is the wide variety of venues and the cross section of peoples he encounters on his visits and talks. The regular diet of Church connections, sporting club connections, youth organisations and educational establishments were spiced in 1993 with a couple of late bookings which provided particularly memorable occasions.

One of these was an invitation to the Annual Presentation Dinner of Birchfield Harriers. Len and Brenda were guests of honour. Len was asked if he could talk for "about 10 minutes."

It was a 'full' evening. There were 49 presentations plus the annual trophy awards to be made after Len had finished talking. The talk was scheduled to cease at 9.30 p.m. After he had been speaking for about 5 minutes, the president passed a slip of paper to him. On it was written "Keep talking Len – as long as you like!" This was a golden moment for Len, who was just about able to keep the talk down to nearly thirty minutes. There was a rapturous reception for him at the end. Subsequently he received several letters from people who were present at the evening but could not get near enough to congratulate him.

The other occasion at the end of 1993 was when he received an invitation from the Governor of H M Prison Featherstone, Wolverhampton, to attend their annual carol concert. Len had addressed the inmates in the autumn that year and he was deeply moved by the warmth of their reception.

'Roger', from the Lifer's group wrote to him and said that during the talk he had gathered that some years before, Len had been presented with an oil painting of the Matterhorn by an artist named Margaret Jinks. Roger continued that he had obtained a picture of the Matterhorn and as he himself did a little painting, he was going to paint the Matterhorn again for Len, and concentrate on capturing the "morning glow" that Len loved so much. Roger ended his letter by writing "Don't hold your breath though Len! Art comes slowly to me, but you will get it, I promise."

At about the same time he received another letter from a different area of the same prison. The following is an extract:

7 December 1993

"Dear Len
How good it was to see you and what a marvellous talk you gave us. I was riveted to my seat and I know, from talking to them, that the others were too. Thankyou seems small praise for the sheer inspiration you gave us all, but when I say it comes from the bottom of our hearts, you can bet it's true.
Sometimes, Len, we can all feel down and that the world is on our shoulders but then someone like you comes along what a tonic it is for us. What motivation to carry on it gives us. Thanks a million from us all. Now Len, on 22 December we have our annual Carol Service in that "lovely Chapel" that you liked so much. Maybe as a special treat (for us) you could bring "the lovely Brenda" who we have heard so much about. What a wonderful woman she must be.................. I really hope that you can make it Len, but will understand if you are already booked up. After hearing your talk we know that there will be a big demand for your company.
Should you not be able to make it Len, may we take this opportunity to wish you and your dear wife all the very best for Christmas and the New Year. May God continue to bless you with the radiance and warmth that you so easily pass on to others.
God Bless Len.
V O'DEA
Head of Inmate Activities"

This set in motion a chain of visits over the next few years during which time Len visited the prison annually. He has developed an innate sensitivity for the prison and its inmates. In particular, the "lifers" group, who have been so grateful to him and, paradoxically, from whom Len has learned so much. He receives a very special welcome from them now, each time he visits. Len contrasts the visits to the prison by remembering the times he has addressed ecumenical gatherings, or the time he addressed the Guild of vergers in the Chapter House at Worcester. Very different venues which produce exactly the same reception from him. This is an important dimension for Len – that groups starting from such different standpoints get the same message.

Chapter Thirty-Two –

ZERMATT

In 1994 Len noticed that many of the picture post-cards on sale in Zermatt bore the name of "Stangier". Knowing that the pilot who flew him to hospital in the helicopter, all those years ago was named Stangier, Len enquired in the area for more information. It seems that 'Sigi' Stangier had started a business in providing the photographs of local scenes for the picture-postcard industry and his name now appears on many of them. In the course of his enquiries, Len found that Sigi was well known for his aerial exploits and daredevil skills. His achievements found wide fame and no doubt contributed to the skill he needed to rescue Len as he did on that occasion. What also delighted Len was to find that Sigi operated from his home address and that was a small hamlet called, believe it or not, FLULEN! As Thomas so cogently put it, "Look Len! You're famous! Your name is on all those cards – He is telling the world that he FluLen from the Matterhorn!"

Sigi had retired from flying and lived alongside Lake Geneva. His photography was as skilful and spectacular as his flying, but sadly, he subsequently died of natural causes at the age of 59.

1994 was a year of more re-unions in fairly rapid succession. Early on, during their holiday that year, Brenda and Len met with Marie-Louise and her family at the 'Alpina'. It was also the year of the guides centenary celebration. Thomas and Len met up, not only with Lucky Imboden, but also his brother Victor. He was the third guide involved in the rescue in 1972. To crown it all, the last evening at the 'Alpina' was marked by dinner with David and Eileen Irvine, of 'Boris Becker shoes' fame. They were staying at the hotel and Len and Brenda enjoyed the last evening in their company. David had been in Australia, covering the tennis news for the "Guardian".

When they returned home, the Yorks spent more time than usual in their garden. It was a particularly fine summer and both Len and Brenda were able to enjoy the fruits of their labours over many years. The garden always looks immaculate and is a constant source of inspiration to Len. He always is generous in praise of Brenda for the time and sheer physical labour that she puts into maintaining its appearance.

Their house in Halesowen was newly built when they moved into it in 1957. The garden has therefore developed, entirely as a result of their own efforts. It was a newly turned-over meadow that had been buried to a depth of several feet with hard clay, by the builder's bulldozer. Today it is a showpiece. Removing fifty cubic yards of clay with pickaxe and wheelbarrow, after work, often with the floodlight on, was "A job of some magnitude," recalls Len. He says this with a wistful glint in his eye, no doubt wishing that he had the chance to tackle it again, without his present-day constraints. He was glad to find the meadow grass and found even that to be something of a trial. In all, the garden preparation took several years before they began the big project that it became. The garden is not enormous in size, but what it lacks in quantity, is surely now compensated by the quality. Very early on, well before Len had even thought about having an accident, he had been able to talk Brenda into agreeing to them having a load of heavy rocks delivered. These water-washed limestone pieces, would emulate, in miniature, the rocks of the Scottish Highlands, to which they were both wedded at the time. The rocks were placed at the top of the garden, to help retain a small terrace and to give the flavour of a distant mountain. What was not envisaged at the time was the degree to which the whole operation would have the opportunity to develop.

Since his fall, and particularly since Len and Brenda have developed their passion for the Swiss landscape, the intended Scottish influence has been replaced by a unique and highly attractive picture of Swiss orientation. The garden falls from its highest point at the site of the rocks, towards the house. Passing through a miniature meadowland slope, bordered by a plantation at the top. "Not easy to mow" says Brenda with a smile – and she should know. She is chief mower. There is a Swiss chalet that serves as a summerhouse and another used

182

for storage. To the right of the garden when viewed from the house, there is a "mountain" stream, designed by Len. The water flows lazily beneath miniature bridges, twists and folds around the profusion of low plants, alpine flowers and bonsai bushes, passing more miniature Swiss chalets *en route*. The whole plot is surrounded by a mix of mature trees, both pine and deciduous. They encircle and protect the site from weather and play host to a plethora of natural fauna.

Lambence at night, lends extra magic.

*　　*　　*　　*　　*

The garden plan is such that it can mostly be viewed from the large picture window of the lounge and Len and Brenda both find it a continuing inspiration. It has also caught the imagination of other, independent people and has featured in the local press regularly. The garden was adjudged to be in the top twenty-five placings in the "Daily Mail" National Garden Competition in 1995. In April 1996 the television company Carlton UK became interested. One or two "glitches" with the timings occurred and consequently a heavy burden of additional work was placed on Brenda to make sure the garden was at the very peak of condition. Eventually an item on the house and garden was included in the programme "Our House". The camera crew covered not only the garden, but the other items of interest throughout the house. They were particularly interested in the pine-clad walls of Len's bedroom. This was designed to resemble the inside of an alpine hut. The huge mural of the Matterhorn on his bedroom wall is so reminiscent of a view of the mountain through a window. Len comments, "In winter, at the first flurry of snow, I can open the window, take a deep breath of the thin air and when the snow flakes waft onto the duvet, I imagine that I am there, in Switzerland, among the superb mountain scenery."

*　　*　　*　　*　　*

Still the individual pieces of the great jigsaw drop into place for Len. In 1997 a letter arrived at Halesowen from Vivienne, the Church

Warden at St Peter's Church, Zermatt, the Church that holds its services in English. Vivienne is indeed English herself and married to a Swiss National. The letter suggested that as it was the twenty-fifth anniversary of Len's accident a special service should be put together on the nearest Sunday to the anniversary date, the twenty-seventh of July. The visiting chaplain at the time of their planned visit, was the Reverend Patrick Duncan. After some correspondence with Patrick the service was arranged and it was with an air of special anticipation that Brenda and Len arrived at Zermatt that year. It was their tenth consecutive visit.

On the morning of the service, breakfast was interrupted by a phone call.

"I'll bet that's for us," said Brenda.

Sure enough, Elizabeth called them. "It's the Chaplain for you," she said, handing the phone to Brenda.

Len's heart sank. "What could have gone wrong for this morning?" he wondered. He had been looking forward to the day for some time and was mildly apprehensive at what Brenda would have to tell him. When she returned, one look at her face was enough to dispel those fears. Wreathed in smiles she announced. "They're out of wine ..... he said ..... could we bring a bottle of red with us for communion!"

Thomas was able to accommodate the chaplain from his cellar and the show was back on the road. St Peters is the church with the gruelling access. There are three flights of difficult zigzag steps. After 15 minutes of climb – Len had made it to the top, Brenda clutching the small bottle of wine.

The service started with the hymn "How Great Thou Art", played by Patrick on the organ. Prayers were lead by Patrick's wife, Sue (herself a Minister). A second hymn followed, "Be Thou my Guardian and my Guide" and then Vivienne set the theme for the service with a reading of Psalm 121, "I will lift up mine eyes unto the hills", a perfect preamble to what was to follow. The Chaplain then introduced Len, who was to address the congregation with his talk "Matterhorn Adventure".

Len stood, and for half an hour spoke and entertained the congregation, conscious that he was standing directly before the holy table, under which were buried the remains of the Reverend Charles Hudson. He had died, as a member of Whymper's party, descending from the top of the Matterhorn, after the first successful climb on 14th July 1865. Len returned to his pew feeling humble and fulfilled at the great honour bestowed upon him by the little church that day. At Len's suggestion, the final hymn was – "Love divine, all loves excelling". The service of thanksgiving had allowed him to say "Thankyou to God" for twenty-five years of happiness and contentment since his accident This, in the sacred place that he would himself have chosen – in the very lea of the mountain.

*   *   *   *   *

A further co-incidence noted by Len and Brenda was that the foundation stone of St Peter's Church was laid on St Peter's Day, 29th June 1869. The church was opened twelve months later – on 29th June 1870. It was seventy years later that St Hilda's Church, Warley Woods (the Church where Brenda and Len worship) was dedicated in 1940. The date was.........29th June.

Their good friends Cathy and Ewan from the Isle of Skye provided the sequel to the holiday in 1997. When the Yorks returned home, waiting for them, as a commemoration of the twenty-five year landmark, sat a bouquet of twenty-five red roses, "Interflora'd" to their home in Halesowen. Len says that they "Bonded their friendship together, much more strongly, than the cement used in the construction of the controversial "Skye Bridge".

Chapter Thirty-Three –

ALAN, JOHN AND CHRISTOPHER

Looking through the picture window, at their beautiful garden, Len has spent some of his most poignant, reflective times recalling his earlier days, particularly those when he was full enough to be leading an almost 'normal' life. (Even in those days, his life-style was slightly removed from the average, when one considers the amount of physical sport to which he subjected himself). His mind would turn to his friend Alan Plant. "As hard as nails and as tough as teak," Len remembers. Alan and Len had covered thousands of miles over the Clent Hills, running together, before he went with Len to the top of the Matterhorn in 1971. He died so early. At the age of forty-nine, struck down by a complaint far removed from his athletic efforts. He was buried in the churchyard at St Kenelm's Church, Clent. His thoughts of Alan would invariably link Len's memory to the days of his earlier youth. To the days when he found it so difficult to make what he wanted of his life because of the limitations imposed on him by his asthmatic tendencies. To the days of "keeping goal because any other position made me out of breath after two minutes of hard running." The days of cricket which he loved so much, to the scouting days when he became "more complete". When his physical prowess improved and he was no longer the sickly child.

Invariably he recalls the characters who served with him in St Hilda's Church Boy Scout Group – Warley Woods 158th – Birmingham. He was eleven years of age when he moved from the warmth and security of the cub pack to the demanding world of 'men'. He was introduced to his patrol leader "Baggy" Winchurch and amongst others, a young man named John Shorthouse. They were men, both of them, 15 years old and a world of challenge and example they set for Len. It was the 'Bulldog' patrol that he had joined and one of their favourite pastimes was to play 'British Bulldog'. This was like playing rugby without a ball, but far more dangerous for an eleven year old. John Shorthouse was built like a prop forward and Len never remembers anyone bringing him down to the ground. 'His' was the side to be on. It was 1938 and soon the rumblings of distant war started to tease away these capable young men. Baggy departed, first of all, to join the RAF as Aircrew. Shortly afterwards, John was also drafted into the RAF and also found to be fit and bright enough to make Aircrew.

Tragically, "Baggy" lost his life, when his plane was shot down, during a bombing raid over Turin.

Meanwhile John led a charmed life and managed to get through the war years. He trained for a time as bomb aimer and was stationed at Bulawayo, Southern Rhodesia. Len was able to obtain, against all the odds, a box of chocolate biscuits. (One of his twin sisters – Abbie – worked for a retailer in Smethwick). Even more amazing, in spite of all the pressures from his sisters, his brothers, not to mention the inordinate number of cousins who came to see him when they heard of the box of chocolates, Len was able to hold on to them long enough to dispatch them to Bulawayo. No doubt, John Shorthouse became an even more popular member of the mess, when he distributed them about the unit. Four years after the second world war had ended, on 26th September 1949, John and his unit were taking part in an exercise that involved hundreds of bombers converging on a target area within a one-hour time span. Two Lancaster bombers collided and all crew perished. Flight Lieutenant John Shorthouse DFM had survived the war, survived being a member of 'Bulldog' patrol, survived playing his beloved 'British Bulldog'.........and had been killed .... taking part in........Operation 'Bulldog'.

The only occasion when he was brought down.

This man of magnetic charm, personality and great physical presence, a man who had played such a big part in developing Len's own character at a crucial time of his life, was dead. At the criminally youthful age of twenty-six years, his remains were laid to rest in the beautiful churchyard at St Kenelm's Church, Clent. His grave is still respected and tended by members of the Halesowen branch of the

Royal Air Forces Association. Len remembers the day of his funeral as one of the most poignant moments of his life. In Len's own words. "On a pleasant October day in 1949, with their friend, the Reverend J C McCallum presiding, a church service was held in St Hilda's, to a packed congregation. (John's family was deeply involved in the life of the church). His mother asked me if I would be a bearer, along with Vernon Williams, Stan Green, John Hambidge and two of John's fellow officers. I will never forget helping to carry John's coffin slowly along the aisle to the NUNC DIMITIS; 'Lord now lettest thy servant depart in peace' – and the chant we sang to the canticle haunts me still. As with Alan Plant, John's remains were interred in St Kenelm's Churchyard, Clent. A spot he loved so much."

*   *   *   *   *

In May 1995 Christopher Reeve, the Superman character most of us will identify with, suffered a fall from a horse when out riding. Whilst the fall was so different to Len's, it soon became apparent that his injuries were very similar in the disability it had caused. After reading one particularly harrowing article, Len was moved to write to him in an effort to help in his recovery. This led to a reply being received. It read:

CHRISTOPHER   REEVE

"Len York   February 1996
Dear Friend
*   Thankyou so very much for your letter of encouragement. Because you took the trouble to write me, I want to tell you how I am and what the future looks like.*
*   I'll admit the first two months after my accident were difficult. I was afraid of being a bother, making people take care of me. But I've found that this isn't about what I've lost – it's about what we can all find in ourselves. When your body doesn't work any more, your mind and spirit must take over. I feel very lucky that I've got the love and support of my family, and friends like you around the*

world. I believe that sometimes things happen for a reason. My job is to discover that reason. And I think I have. <u>If I can help people understand that this can happen to anyone, anytime, then maybe it's all worthwhile.</u> I know I can make a difference in the way Americans look at spinal chord injury and paralysis. I've been invited by the American Paralysis Association to take part in raising money for research into spinal chord injuries. We need to find ways to prevent these injuries and to return those who suffer from them to productive lives. I know it can be done. My doctor has told me about some dramatic evidence of progress. For example a protein that inhibits spinal chord growth has been identified. But we are not doing enough in this country. In fact, Congress may be heading away from funding research. Today, in the United States, there are a quarter of a million people like me, most of them young men injured in sports or automobile accidents. Our nation spends billions of dollars a year to maintain us. It'll take about $400,000 a year just to care for me, one person.

I think it is far more cost effective to invest funds in research that can help cure us than to keep spending money on caretaking. I hope you will join me in the biggest fight of my life. Please write your Congress person. And if you can send a donation to the American Paralysis Association, that would be great. I assure you that your donation will help push the search for new, successful treatments to the next level.

I see tremendous opportunities and potential in my life. I take genuine joy in every moment I'm alive. And I want you to know that your letter meant so much to my family and me, at a time when it would have been easy to lose hope. With your help, I know there is a bright and promising future for me and everyone like me.

We're going to make it!"
Sincerely
The letter was signed by Dana M Reeve (Christopher's wife)

It was a letter that could have been written, word for word, by Len himself. The last paragraph could have come verbatim from one of Len's own talks. It prompted Len to reply:

190

12 3 96

"Dear Christopher Reeve

When your letter arrived, Tuesday 5th March I was on the way out into Birmingham to give my slide show "Matterhorn Adventure" to the Walsall Probus Club (Retired Professional and businessmen). I just had to stop everything, sit down and read it after noticing the USA postmark!

The contents of your letter gave me tremendous joy and happiness. Your positive approach to the serious spinal injury you suffered shines like a beacon in the gloom and must give hope to many. I was able to read your letter to my audience, much to their pleasure, and the expenses they gave me that morning I joyfully send to the "American Paralysis Association".

I was very fortunate to get on my feet again after my 'broken neck' at 13,000 feet on the Matterhorn and have been able to travel all over England with my 'lecture' which has resulted in many hundreds of pounds going to the spinal injuries unit at the Orthopaedic Hospital, Oswestry, where I spent eight happy months in 1972-73

Like yourself, I am blessed with a positive attitude and consider my gains far outweigh my losses, and genuinely feel Our Lord has been good to me! Again, like you, I am blessed with a caring wife and family and friends, without whom life would be impossible, but with them I can conquer the World!

I can drive again using hand controls, walk a little with crutches, but this enables me to keep busy with my 'Matterhorn show' and to visit other spinal injury victims, inspiring them to fight!

I would not change my life with anyone and I also take genuine joy in every moment I'm alive.

May God bless you, your Wife and Family in the battle lying ahead!

To echo your own words: We're going to make it!
Yours sincerely
Len York" – the signature was accompanied by the pen drawing that is now synonymous with Len's signature – the amusing figure of a man skipping down the Matterhorn, singing.

191

Within days of their correspondence – on 26th March 1996, pictures of Christopher Reeve appeared in the American national press. He had attended the 'Oscar' ceremony in Hollywood. He took the stage in a wheelchair, addressed the gathering and received a five-minute standing ovation from the stars gathered there. He left many of them with tears streaming down their faces. Robin Williams said "The auditorium was filled with stars, but Chris shone the brightest."

Chapter Thirty-Four –

GLEN OF WEEPING

Over many years of giving talks to groups of Boys' Brigade members, a special relationship developed between Len and the members of 5th West Bromwich Company. They honoured him by asking if he would join them at their camps in North Wales and Anglesey on several occasions. He was able to accept their kind invitations for three separate camps, getting so much from being able to sleep again, in a tent, on hard floors at times, but always with a great sense of comradeship and mutual enjoyment.

In 1983, to mark the Centenary Celebration of the Boys Brigade, the 5th West Bromwich Company asked Len to join them in a presentation evening, to be staged in a hotel in Walsall. There were many awards to their members and towards the end of the evening they rocked Len by presenting him with a booklet they had produced, listing many of his achievements since his fall. Len was deeply touched that they had gone to so much trouble to put it together, "And what a good job they have made of it," he was heard to enthuse. What he was told next, almost had him jumping from his seat. The Company had kept a second copy for their file and a third copy had been sent to Jimmy Saville at the TV headquarters for the programme "Jim' ll Fix It". They wrote about Len's history and suggested that Len would be proud to take part in anything that could be organised to enable him to fly, by helicopter, around the Matterhorn, or to repeat the journey he took in the rescue helicopter in 1972.

For reasons best known to the organisers of the programme, it couldn't be "fixed" but it seems that Len was destined to make the acquaintance of Sir Jimmy Saville OBE at a later date.

In late April 1999 an envelope dropped through the letterbox at Len and Brenda's home in Halesowen. It was from the Robert Jones

193

and Agnes Hunt Orthopaedic & District Hospital NHS Trust. It read:

> *Dear Mr York*
>
> *You are cordially invited to the laying of the foundation stone of the new spinal Injuries Centre on Thursday 20th May 1999.*
>
> *We are delighted that Sir Jimmy Saville, OBE, has agreed to join us on what will undoubtedly be a very memorable occasion for the Robert Jones & Agnes Hunt Orthopaedic and District Hospital.*
>
> *Whilst we have made excellent progress with the Appeal which now stands at £3.15m, to raise the remaining £400k is still a demanding challenge.*
>
> *The support we have received to date has been quite overwhelming and we will continue in our efforts to attract new donors....................*

The letter continued, and was signed by W.S. El Masry, FRCS Ed Consultant in Spinal Injuries and Gwilym Owen OBE. Appeal Director.

It was customary of the Spinal Unit to invite Len and Brenda to any of their special functions. Len was always seen as one of their rather special achievements and they respect the fact that he calls at the Unit regularly to talk to the patients and to do what he does best – to inspire them to make the most of their disabilities.

Of course he was delighted at the prospect of meeting the man who had spent so much of his time raising money for the Stoke Mandeville Hospital in the past.

The occasion gave Len the opportunity to have a long talk with Jimmy. Always being interested in Scotland, Len ventured to ask Jimmy where he lived and when he found it was in the heart of the Highlands that meant so much to both of them, they had things to discover together.

Jimmy described to Len, where in Glencoe he lived but that was not enough. Len asked for more detail, because there was a glimmer of recognition in his eye as Jimmy described the location.

"Well now," said Len, "That amazes me, where you are describing sounds to me just like the house where Hamish MacInnes lives."

Jimmy was visibly amused at the detection of this fellow. "You're spot on!" he responded. "Hamish did live there, he sold the house to me some years ago."

"Well, I don't believe it," Len continued, with incredulity etched in every line of his wrinkled face. "When Brenda and me were courting.... now.... there's an old fashioned word for you Jim.... we rode our Claude Butler tandem," (Jim was already smiling again at the recollection of those 'Good old days') "to the very house you describe. We wanted to walk in the local hills and I decided to knock at the door of that residence to enquire if the owner would mind if we left the bike against his side wall." When the door opened and Hamish MacInnes stood on the step I couldn't believe my eyes. He was most gracious and permission was immediately granted. I asked him which was the best route to the 'Lost Valley'. He directed us and wished us a good day! When he turned to go back inside, he could have been going back into his workshop to work on one of his famous inventions for all I know. But what I did know, was that I had shaken hands with one of my all-time heroes that day."

Jimmy Saville listened to the story probably closer than Len thought. Len was minded of the time when Jimmy Saville was an international road race cycling personality. That was before his days as a radio and TV presenter.

The two cyclists continued to swap stories about their biking years and time passed quickly, as it always does when two protagonists are closely engrossed in a consuming interest. Len warmed to this extrovert character. Perhaps he saw something of himself in the enthusiasm of the man. Here was someone who was a 'big' character in every sense of the word. He had time for everyone at the spinal unit; patients, ex-patients, staff, domestics, surgeons, administrators, visitors. They all got the same treatment from Jim. They saw knock-about humour, irreverent posturing and above all, a genuine interest in all that was happening and the people who were making it happen. No doubt these attributes had contributed to Sir James being honoured by the Queen.

Len and Brenda had enjoyed their day with the spinal unit and were delighted to learn that there would be a follow-up visit during 2001, when it was planned to have the unit completed.

*   *   *   *   *

Some months later a package arrived at Len's home. It was addressed to Mr Charles Leonard York, from Glencoe Productions Ltd, Glencoe, Argyll and read:

> *Dear Charles*
> *Jimmy Saville gave me copies of your accident details from your*
> *Matterhorn encounter – and also your connections with Glencoe.*
> *In fact I remember you at my home in Glencoe all those years ago....*
> *I have enclosed a reminder of the Glen and hope that you enjoy it.*
> *Best wishes*
> *   Hamish MacInnes*

The 'reminder of the Glen' was a television production by Hamish. It was called "Palin's Progress and the Glen of Weeping". It showed Michael Palin crossing the notorious Aonach Eagach Ridge in Glencoe, the narrowest ridge on the British mainland – and in winter.

With his son, Tom and Sherpa guide, Ang Pherba, Michael again displayed his qualities as the intrepid explorer.

The camaraderie that prompted this action from Jimmy Saville and Hamish MacInnes meant the entire world to Len.

And always will.

Chapter Thirty-Five –

THE JOURNEY CONTINUES

Brenda stood in the lounge, running her eyes over the garden, the line of the stream, the chalets, and rocks. She mentally checked off the jobs that would need doing before winter set in. Certainly the lawn needed to be cut, probably twice more, before it would be safe to stow away the mower for another winter. The morning dew clung heavily to the blades of grass. Even with the sun doing its best to evaporate the bejewelled beads, it was fighting a progressively losing battle. Soon the lawns would hold the droplets all day, as the September mornings opened with heavier mists and the battle of the sun would become impossible. It had been a disappointing summer in some ways. Following several years of warm sunshine that everyone in the British Isles had taken to be the harbinger of warmer summers to come, the elements had lapsed once more into their old frustrating ways. The years 1998, 1999 and 2000 had produced sunshine, cloud and showers in fairly equal proportions, but usually at the wrong time and in the wrong quantities. "No doubt that is why the garden has looked so special this year," she thought aloud. A positive thought that Len himself would have been proud of.

It was a morning when Len had a meeting with the St Kenelm's Church congregation at Clent. It was some years since he had talked to the Mother's Union, and the committee felt it time for him to update them. Len always seemed able to weave the latest twists of fate into the story of the 'miracle' of his life.

It was years since Brenda had heard Len do his talk, although she always knew what he put into them. Hadn't she for years, until her recent retirement, typed the items for his scrap book? She had made dozens of copies of his many newspaper cuttings, referring to himself and to the many friends he had gathered along the way. Didn't she know him "like a book", and wasn't she able to predict the things he would do and say more often than not? Didn't this follow from so many years of helping, watching, prompting, arguing, cajoling, loving him? Despite Len not referring to a note when delivering his talk, she reckoned she could be sure of knowing seventy-five percent of what he would say.

That morning, for reasons unknown to her, she decided the other twenty-five per cent was worth listening to. It was a beautiful morning, he wouldn't start the talk until 11 a.m. and she hadn't been to Clent for years, although they could see it from their home. They both had such warm feelings of 'belonging' because of their connections when children. For Len, the place had even stronger ties because the remains of two of his very best friends, coincidentally, lay in the churchyard. Neither Alan Plant nor John Shorthouse had ever met so far as Len was aware but both had had a profound effect on Len's life and both were figures remembered with great affection by Len and Brenda. One had stood with Len at the pinnacle of his physical achievement and the other was with him at his spiritual pinnacle.

"Yes, that decides it," she thought, "If I want to hear Len talk, where better than Clent?"

*   *   *   *   *

There were plenty of cars parked on the car park near the top of the churchyard and Brenda had to tuck her's next to Len's. His was the only car parked at the Lych Gate entrance further down the lane. Looking down on her from above the Lych Gate stood the sentinel figure of St Kenelm. This Prince of Mercia was said to have been murdered and died at the spot where the well sprung. The water has run in the church grounds ever since. She looked up, smiled at the carving and said, "Do excuse me – but there were no parking spaces up the lane."

She walked through the gate and down the steep path to the church door. The wired portico was open but she had to lift the latch on the heavy solid timber door. With a deft twist of the mechanism, she had gained entrance to the cool, dimly lit church. Allowing a moment for her eyes to become adjusted to the dim light, she moved silently to one of the pews near the door, some way from the gathered members at the front of church. The light was more restricted than normal because of the extra curtaining employed as "blackout" at the windows. This was to give Len a better platform for his slides.

Len's attention was being held by the lady speaker who had just introduced him and who was a little embarrassed as to whether Len would stand or sit for his talk. He failed to notice Brenda's entrance and she was glad – she would not want him to feel inhibited at her presence.

The opening was typical – Len spotted the problem the lady was having and took charge – "I'll stand if it's all the same to you – it's therapeutic." As he spoke he gathered the two sticks that had rested against the arms of his chair since he dropped himself into the seat about twenty minutes earlier. He pushed himself into the upright position as he spoke and adopted his slightly hunched stance. He beamed at the audience. "I know you're feeling sorry for me" he said "but we shall soon put a stop to that!" The awkward moment was over. The congregation, some of whom who had heard him before, laughed and relaxed in their chairs. Those who hadn't heard him before smiled, slightly more self-consciously, wondering what they had let themselves in for.

"We can't afford to waste a moment of this wonderful life can we?" he asked his audience, involving them from the very moment of rising to his feet. "You may know that I hold two areas of the world very close to me, that's why I'm wearing my Lindsay tartan trousers and Matterhorn shirt. On the 29th June 1940, as a choirboy with St Hilda's Church Warley – and I am still a member of that same choir," he confirmed, "I learned the old authorised version of Psalm 121 – I will lift up my eyes," everyone in the church joined him at this point and together they chanted "to the hills. From whence commeth my help? My help cometh from the Lord who made Heaven and Earth." The congregation stopped at this point but Len went on alone "He will not suffer thy foot to be moved. But you will say 'Ah but He did with you Len,' but He didn't – not with any animosity! What He did do, was to guide me through a window of life that made me the happiest man in the world," he hesitated whilst looking squarely at the audience, then continued. "And there is nowhere I would rather be in sharing that happiness than here, at Clent, with you, today. Looking around at your faces, bursting with anticipation....." The audience caught the innuendo and the laughter was now audible. *It's often a little fraught at this point," said Len, "I go all over the country talking to people like this and often at this stage, I am the only relaxed person in the room." He beamed at them again and they were with him now – they knew they were in for an hour or so of rare entertainment.

"If the Queen, the President of the United States of America, the Archbishop of Canterbury walked into this church now, I would have no difficulty talking to them – I would be quite at ease. I wouldn't have been at ease before my accident. We put people on pedestals and when we find out the truth about them, it makes us feel like saints – the things they get up to. I am sure we all have moral principles, but they don't always seem to."

"Now – where was I........ yes......... Psalm 121. And that is why I tell you that I am the happiest man in the world. Oh! I suspect I see some doubting faces." He adjusted his stance on his sticks so that if it became necessary to emphasise a point, he could raise his stick in the air. It lent much more emphasis than stabbing at the audience with a finger. "You say, Oh! he must have fallen on his head! – Well I did!" He had to stop at this point because of the volume of laughter and as they subsided he revitalised them with "And it did me a favour!"

"Let me give you a piece of advice." The audience quietened down now to pick up the next gem. "I always say, if you are going to have an accident," and the audience who had attended before were in front of him now, already tittering, "have a darned good one! If in life you are destined to break your neck, see if you can pick a spot better than the one I chose."

He was getting well into his stride and kept the attention of the audience by saying, "I was a mountaineer for 30 or 40 years. A road-runner doing up to eighty miles a week. A keen cyclist and a long distance walker. I could have chosen any venue, but I chose to fall from a Mountain Ridge at 13000 feet on the finest Mountain in the world. A wonderful spot and I can tell you that if it should happen to you or something like it, you will thank the Lord for every day you live afterwards. I wonder how many fit people stop to say 'Thankyou' to God for every day that they are enjoying a normal life – not many I'll bet. But you do when you have broken your neck. Twenty-six years ago I had my accident and I have since had twenty-six years of joy and pleasure. It gave me a purpose for living – there really is a God. Look what he has done for Len – standing here, smiling. Yet I couldn't get to that table without my sticks."

"I could be at home watching television, reading the paper, concentrating on my photography, but I am happier having the time of my life here with you." This was the inspirational Len that people had gathered to hear. "I don't feel disabled – to be honest I haven't a pain in my body. I feel like I do when I am addressing a group of school children. I am one of them. You don't get old yourself, do you? It's the person sitting next to you who's getting old!" The audience looked at each other and threw their hands in the air at this one and it took a few moments for the sheer enjoyment on Len's face to subside with his audience so completely hyped up. "On my next birthday I must confess I shall be seventy-four!"

"It doesn't matter how wealthy you are. The richest man in the world cannot go to the supermarket and say 'I'll have that box of contentment you're selling up there." He raised his left stick at that point to emphasise the position of the product on the imaginary supermarket shelf. "It is impossible to buy it – and I have an abundance of it!......contentment.

But there is a price to pay for the contentment that I share with you all.... and who pays that price?.....It's my dear wife Brenda." At this point Brenda felt an involuntary shiver down the length of her spine. She wondered if the earth was about to open up under her. She had not listened to his talk for years and had not been prepared for this. Had he seen her? Surely not – he wouldn't have embarrassed her to this extent – and no one in the church knew her – did they? She wondered if it had been such a good idea after all to come unannounced, but her husband continued.

"Brenda is the one who has carried the cross for me these last twenty-six years, but the Lord has provided Brenda with a shoulder to cope.

201

Not only to cope with me, but with a very responsible full time job, two cars, a house and a fantastic garden that has been featured on National Television twice recently." The master paused again, and this was becoming a sign to his audience that something special was coming........ "For three minutes twenty two seconds the first time, and two minutes the second time." The laughter broke the spell and Brenda relaxed again. She was sure now that he had not seen her. He would certainly not have referred to her without telling the audience had he known she was sitting near the door.

"Don't laugh," said Len to the congregation, "You can do a lot in five minutes, can't you? When I went to tell my friend Freddie at Rifflealp, he said, 'Three minutes and two minutes Len – you are famous. When the TV crew came here to film the Matterhorn and my restaurant they only gave me five seconds!"

Len remembered where he had left his talk and came back to it by saying, "Brenda's the one who bears my cross and He helps her because she needs it more than most. That's what is so wonderful about the Lord. If you need to call on Him – He is there. But if you don't need him, He doesn't interfere. Isn't that wonderful? And He forgives us – if I'm a sinner, I tell him I'll be good tomorrow – and mean it – and He forgives me."

"Well my friends," said Len, as if to signify the end of the sermon, (and he was after all speaking to the converted), "I'm going to take you to the top of the Matterhorn twice and have a quick look at the North Face of The Eiger..... my, you are all looking so excited about that!" His own enthusiasm teased another laugh from his audience but they knew they were in for more humour yet; he was just getting into his stride as his thoughts turned to the meat of his talk.

"In 1971, I stood, with 3 of my friends from the West Bromwich Mountaineering Club, on the top of the Matterhorn, in the footprints of Edward Whymper who first climbed to the top in 1865. It is the most beautiful of mountains. We shook hands, embraced and said 'Thankyou God for the experience and fulfilment of a lifetime'. So humble, so thrilled. At the bottom, after carefully negotiating the descent, we embraced again, shook hands and said 'Never again!' Twelve months later I was standing in the same footprints – but the Lord controls our destiny."

"What had happened was that my employers had said, 'Len, after 25 years long and loyal service as Chief Draughtsman, you can have five days extra holiday' – Ain't that marvellous! I went home, told Brenda – she was delighted too – she said 'You will be able to go climbing if you like!' – Isn't that marvellous! You think to yourself 'Well if my wife's happy for me to go climbing, what the devil is *she* going to do?' But I'd got Brenda's blessing! I went to the 'Globe Inn', Reform St, West Bromwich that very same night – where the West Bromwich Mountaineers still meet, and a note passed from hand to hand. It offered a three-week trip to the Alps, taking in the Eiger, Mont Blanc and the Matterhorn at a cost of £27. £27 for three weeks. Remember that figure 'cos it's important! – you can't take your wife out for a meal these days for that money! Three weeks of the most fantastic three peaks in Europe for £27 – I thought, God you have dealt me four aces. Isn't that marvellous?"

"My name went down on the top of the list – £5 non-returnable deposit paid! Brenda's blessing, time off, £5 paid. Cheap trip. All unplanned!" He paused; eyes shining, corners of his mouth slightly turned up anticipating the pleasure to come as he would return to this point, knowing from experience it was a winner with the audience every time.

"Set off, July 1972 for the Eiger. Fifty-four seater coach, twenty-nine climbers, almost two seats each. Two and a half days to Grindelwald."

"Now, the Eiger don't look too bad on a six-inch postcard! It's the next day, when you open the door of your tent, and you see a mile high vertical north face climbing into the heavens. We were going the easy way, but the easy way looked anything but easy! We didn't make it and had to content ourselves with some exercises on the lower slopes to prepare us for the rest of the trip."

"We then set off for the Matterhorn, arriving in Zermatt in superb weather. Now you know that Brenda and I, between us, have had fifteen holidays in Zermatt, – almost without a cloud. We have been thirty-eight times to Scotland, sometimes twice a year – and invariably get good weather. So the moral is – go when I go, and go where I go."

"The perfect weather held while we climbed to the Hornli Hut at the bottom of the Matterhorn. The hut is at 10,500 feet. Three times the height of Snowdon and you are at the bottom of the climb. Anyone who can walk well can make it – there's a good track – it's all uphill! If you want a little outing one weekend, ladies – I can thoroughly recommend it! There's a tea shop at this point!" This brought an appreciative chuckle from his audience at the prospect. "The bit above the Hornli Hut requires care." he continued, "It is the height of Ben Nevis – but there is no tourist track to the top!"

"We were booked in at the hut for the night and practised our climbing on the lower slopes until late that evening before going to bed at about ten o'clock. Bed was a blanket on the floor but don't be too worried about the discomfort 'cos you don't stay too long anyway.

A voice, at 2 a.m. says 'If you are climbing the Matterhorn get up now – it is 2 am. and a perfect day.' How does he know it's a perfect day? It's two o'clock in the morning; it is pitch black and bitterly cold! Breakfast is eaten at half-past two in the morning. We had a Swiss meusli mix. Now that's not too bad at 8.30 in the morning – and even better with milk. But the milkman don't deliver at ten and a half thousand feet at two in the morning and the water is frozen. So we mixed our orange juice with the mix. It was revolting! But my friends....... you've gotta eat! Our next meal was to be seventeen hours later. We went all day on orange juice and muesli – I can recommend it if you want to put yourself to some torture!"

"So out into the darkness at 3am – and it *is* dark. No street lamps, no signposts, just this naked rock climbing up into the darkness and cold – really cold."

"We were talking to the Lord in a way – but not in a very complimentary way. We were saying 'God, why are we doing this?' But the Lord answered. At a quarter to five. By lighting the tip of the mountain above us, with the most beautifully radiant deep red-gold luminescence. It gradually creeps its way down.....unmasking the shape of the mountain, slowly..... whilst the world below is still in complete darkness. The rock is a golden glow. At this point you say, 'Thankyou God, this is why we climb – for the beauty of the Earth!"

"That day, we stood on the top of the mountain at half-past one. For me it was the second time in twelve months and it was magic! We were four hours later than the year before. My camera recorded the scene, to prove to Brenda that my £27 had been well spent! After one hour on the summit we started our descent. At 6.30 we were at the Solvay hut. It was Sunday night and Evensong would be starting back at home. We were still at 13,200 feet. We couldn't stay there because my pal George, to whom I was roped, was getting married and his wife to be, Francis, was waiting at the bottom. If we hadn't gone down that night, can you imagine what she would have thought – she'd have thought we had had an accident, or worse still, that George wasn't coming back. So, it was reluctantly that we said goodbye to the cosmopolitan crowd in that little shed. We couldn't stay – we had to put in an appearance. We abseiled from the hut doorway and at 7.30 p.m. we were at 12,500 feet, stopping for food, for the first time in seventeen hours. We hadn't thought of eating up to this point. We were so excited. We were enjoying ourselves so much! I am sure we often eat out of sheer boredom. Between 7.30 and 8 p.m. we ate chocolate and dates washed down with water that had been collected as snow from the top of the mountain.

"I thought to myself, it's Sunday – 7.40 p.m. The choir will probably be recessing down the aisle at St Hilda's. I wonder if they are playing one of my favourite hymns. It's one that many of you will know from wedding ceremonies – 'Love divine all loves excelling, Joy of heaven to earth come down' – to the tune of Blaenwern. But enough of this! I said out loud to George, we have 2 hours of daylight left and two thousand feet to descend. We must go!"

"George started to move into gear as he roped up to me again. Slowly, we re-packed our rucksacks. Then I saw George safely down about 30 feet of the face. It was steep rock with plenty of footholds and plenty of handholds. For a few moments I wasn't watching George, I found the views to right and left preferable to watching his backside disappearing down a rock face."

"George slipped. I didn't have a split second. The rope went taught and I was pulled off headfirst from my chest harness. I hurtled one hundred and twenty feet down the east face of the Matterhorn at twelve and a half thousand feet and God, you don't half go fast. I learnt at Smethwick Tech. all those years ago that a body falls at thirty-two feet per second squared. Now, that don't sound fast when you say it but I can assure you – you don't half go fast, hurtling down the face."

The audience had gone quiet during the relating of the last few sentences, apart from an occasional gasp or a sharp withdrawing of breath from one or two who were living the moment that happened so long ago. So graphic, in the words of one of the protagonists.

The transportation was complete – *a long way from Clent.*

Len waited a practised few seconds and then broke the spell by saying, "Then the Lord came to my aid. You ask, 'How Len?' Well, I landed headfirst! You can thank the Lord for that!" He was beaming again at the noise of the audience laughing. They relaxed momentarily before immediately being dragged up the mountain again by the speaker, whose face took on a serious countenance, as he progressed his story.

"You can thank the Lord for that," he repeated, "because I went into a coma! I was then unconscious for the next twelve hours of my life. The miracle of the fall was that the rope held and supported me when I was at the end of the one hundred and twenty-foot length of it. I was there, in a coma with a broken neck. I dangled at the end of a rope with a two thousand foot drop below me – but dead to this world." The pregnant silence was broken again by him, using words utterly typical, he said – "Wasn't *that* good!"

The audience was not sure at this point. They retrenched into a respectful silence, waiting for the next morsel.

"What about George? Thankfully, he slipped only a short distance and stopped. He looked up in time to see me hurtling past him, through space, obviously horrified. He took a stance. Apparently, it held. I don't know – I can only tell you what he told me and what others have expressed as opinions. What I *do* know is that George then had the task of climbing down to where my silent body was swinging. He thought I was dead!" The pause was again used to effect here. "He hadn't known me to be quiet in his life before!"

"He listened ..... no sound from Len. He climbed down. Pulled me onto a ledge, bound me tightly on with a climbing rope and shouted 'Len – we've had an accident – I am going for help!' I couldn't hear him. But he didn't know that. He then had to leave me. On a ledge, at eight o'clock at night. Alone. With a broken neck that he didn't know about. Cut and bruised, with a head wound that needed sixteen stitches. Torn clothing." He gave impetus to the point by indicating the position of the tear in his clothes. "He wrapped me up in a thin red anorak so that I could be spotted easily. Then he made his way down the face. Now .... just after he left...... it started to hail!" One member of his audience let out an involuntary "Oh" at this point and others "tutted" or let out a resigned gasp.

"Now remember, I was alone and probably inadequately dressed for a hailstorm. My friends, I can get bronchitis easier than you can get on a bus! How I survived that night I shall never know!"

"George, bless him was meanwhile getting down that two thousand feet and by ten o'clock, he burst into the Hornli hut, raised the alarm, and almost immediately three tough Swiss Alpine guides and a young nurse named Marie Louise set off up the mountain. In the darkness, to try and locate me. If you have ever tried to keep up with mountain rescue-fit people, you will know what a test it is. They are invariably seven feet tall, as broad as oxen and toughness itself. Their rate of ground coverage requires a tremendous degree of fitness, just to stay with them. I marvel at the courage of this young girl for even attempting to go with them. Not a trained mountaineer – but a nurse! God I shall always be grateful to you for sending Marie Louise to my aid!"

"Because George had given them a good guide as to where I was, they found me, almost frozen to death, at midnight. I'd had four hours on the mountain alone. Can you imagine what I would have thought if I had woken up when I was alone? Paralysed from the neck down, unable to feel anything, unable to move anything. Does anyone know I am here?"

"I would have died from fright!"

"Anyway, I was found. As it was midnight, two of the guides went back down to the Hornli hut to raise the alarm for a helicopter rescue at first light. The chief guide and Marie-Louise spent the night with me. They wrapped me in warmer clothing and stayed with me from midnight to a quarter to five – first light. At a quarter to five a noisy helicopter arrived and suspended a net below it. Then I was apparently got inside the net and hoisted up beneath the helicopter – not inside

207

– and the pilot flew away. I was apparently swinging about underneath – just like a bag of sprouts in the early dawn, as we left the Matterhorn." The listeners were entranced by the details of the rescue. This light-hearted reference was just what they wanted to bring them back down to earth. They were ready for more lightheartedness and Len sensed it.

"Now – I don't object to the £300 it cost to pick me off by helicopter but do you remember some minutes ago; I told you I had gone on the trip because I had been offered a cheap £27 costing?" There was a ripple of laughter and Len sensed that more humour was needed.

"And the expense is only just beginning. If I could have called up to the pilot, I would have shouted 'Take me home and I will have it done on the National Health! Instead, he flew me to the most expensive hospital he could find in Berne. I have found out since that it's a lot cheaper to die in the Alps than it is to get over a broken neck! Tragically, the cemetery in Zermatt is full of graves of people who did not have the chance. They died on the Matterhorn. No chance of recovering."

"One hundred and twenty-five pounds a day to stay in the hospital, in 1972! Not a lot today is it?" queried Len.

"It's still a lot today if you haven't got it!" The voice came from the audience. They were obviously beginning to enjoy themselves at the constant referring to the cost of things, so Len decided to let them have more.

"In 1972 you could live for twelve months on £125." countered Len. "You could live forever! And another thing I've discovered since – in 1972 you could have had a flight – *inside* the helicopter – around the Matterhorn – for £25. So why did I have to pay £300 for a trip – without a seat – outside the plane?" It took a little while to stop them laughing.

"I woke up after twelve hours. I was in a spotless ward of a wonderful hospital. Top floor suite. Crisp, clean sheets. When I woke up I did not feel too bad. I could open my eyes and the rest of me did not seem to be in pain. I wasn't sure why I was in bed. I did not know that if you're paralysed you don't get the sensation of pain. That's why I can laugh with you today - I have no pain. It's no laughing matter when I get toothache — I can feel that!"

"When I woke, the Doctor came to me and said I had had a fall on the Matterhorn. He said I had a broken neck. I said to him, Doctor, let me tell you. Matterhorn, eight o'clock Sunday night. East face. I fell. I didn't slip Doc. Is it Monday morning, about eight o'clock?"

He said "It is eight o'clock, it is Monday, and I just cannot believe you! You have a broken neck and may not walk again. You have been in a coma for twelve hours and yet you don't seem to have lost anything of your perception."

"I said to him, Doctor, I just don't feel too bad! When I went to sleep on the Matterhorn, I could walk fifty miles. I could run marathons. I had climbed the Matterhorn before. Now if I develop an itch, I cannot scratch myself. I can't move. I was in trouble and I realised it then. I would have swopped that bed then with anyone. People say 'Len you're so brave..... but there's no bravery to it when you're confined to the bed and can't move. It's Hobson's choice. Bravery is when you have a chance to run away from a problem and you choose to stay with it. George, Marie Louise, the Guides come immediately to mind." The audience had fallen into serious mood again – time to change tack, thought Len.

"If a roaring Lion walked into this room now – you could all run off." He shuffled uncomfortably on his crutches to emphasise his problem and the audience responded immediately. Len's face lit up again as he continued. "I would have to talk to it – or pat it's mane!"

"When the doctor made it clear to me – I was scared. The next line he used made me forget I was paralysed – they have this way of making you forget your problems don't they?" he asked rhetorically. Then with a sly look at the audience, he delivered the punch line – "The doctor said, 'we have been trying to contact your wife!"

"I said, have you got to tell her?"

The doctor countered "I am asking her to fly over immediately."

"Fly?" Len said, looking as hurt as he could muster, with no movement in his limbs. "Doctor, do you realise I came over here on a cheap £27 ticket which has already cost me the best part of £400. Have I got to pay for Brenda's flight as well? He was a nice man in a white coat!" The audience was enjoying it again now, "My God I *was* scared when I knew that Brenda was coming – it removed all fear of my broken neck – I was scared to death at what Brenda would say!"

From her hidden spot, in the darkness, Brenda smiled with the audience. She knew this fellow of old. There wasn't a malicious thought in his head, but he would have found it difficult she supposed, if she had been of the mind to put him "on the spot" over his antics in her absence. In fact, she remembered, he was far too injured to remonstrate with at the time and she certainly had not gone for that purpose. She was enjoying his performance hugely, and wondered how she would extricate herself without him knowing she had been present. If she could get away with it she could have great fun with him later!

He allowed his audience to settle again before admitting to them. "Nothing was really funny then. Everything is funny now because I can stand here and tell you about it – but I did not know what would happen to me then." He thought for a moment, "Look at Superman – Christopher Reeve, he only fell off a horse and he will never stand in front of an audience again – not according to the medical profession's current state of understanding of paralysis.

Now there's a brave man. Because of his commitment, it was a relatively short time until he could sit in a wheelchair at the Oscar Ceremony. He must have worked very hard to achieve that in so short a time, but he has accepted that the wheelchair is his friend and that he will find it difficult to progress from there. I am glad that with me, it has been a long, steady job. I thank the Lord that it has been as successful as it has been. I visit youngsters regularly aged seventeen, eighteen or so. They have broken their necks diving into swimming pools or in car accidents. They have to sit in a chair and have everything done for them. If they want a cup of tea, the nurse brings it along and puts it by the side of them. Then they have to wait until someone else brings them a straw. They cannot so much as pick up the cup to their lips.

If I want a cup of tea I can pick it up to my lips and enjoy it. Their only hope is that there will be a medical development, a miracle that will mean a spinal chord can be mended. Can you see why I thank God for my mobility? It may not seem much to a normal person, but to me, the level of my independence means everything!"

"Now that you have all seen me, do you mind if I sit down?" The switch of emphasis again relieved the pressure on the audience. Len had been standing fully for three-quarters of an hour. "Now where had I got to?" – another rhetorical question that no one bothered to answer. They were used to him by now. He hadn't referred to a script in all this time – Brenda knew he didn't have a script. If anyone had typed one out for him, it would have been her.

"Oh yes – Brenda – the Doctor told me that they had traced her through the local police to East Anglia where she had gone to see her sister. Do any of you know East Anglia?" While posing the question he extended his hand towards them, palm down, and waved it across his chest emphasising a flat surface. "Flat as a pancake. If you want to climb in East Anglia, you have to go up to bed!" He angled the flat hand in a series of ascending steps. "So Brenda came after four days. It would have been three but she missed the plane. She had to go home to Halesowen as her mother was with her. She had to pick up her clothes and get down to Gatwick. But in all the rush and not being used to plane travel, she got too late for the plane. She had to wait another twenty-four hours for the next one."

"Do you know what it was like in the hospital? Probably the best hospital in the world for my particular type of injury, and with such a wonderful staff. ....It was lonely. I was immobilised. Lying on my back, my body in a plaster cast up to my neck. Looking at a ceiling that was costing £125 a day. From the corner of my eye I could see a clock on the wall. It had a second-hand and every second seemed like a week and every minute was like a year for the first few days. But while Brenda was on her way, on the very day when she missed her plane, the Lord sent an Angel to me. The Angel's halo appeared above my face while I lay there. It was about three feet across and had a veil hanging from it. The Angel spoke to me in English. She said, in a small voice, 'Mr York, I hope you don't mind me coming to see you in your trouble, but I saw a report in the local paper about your accident. My mother was an English lady – she died in this hospital. She said this not in a way to frighten me, but in explanation – in a conversational way. She was wearing a hat that would have done justice to the Italian nuns who you see about. A very wide brimmed hat, hung with a see through veil. This, combined with the sun shining through it gave her the appearance of an angel in my half asleep state. She was a devout

Roman Catholic, a woman of fantastic faith and she came to see me and Brenda every day I was in hospital. Now you see why she was an angel? Her daily visits and her letters for eight years afterwards, kept me going. They still support me today. An extra crutch that enables me to stand before you today."

"Her name was Ruth Brozy!"

"I am pleased that God chose me, from all the spinal victims, to be able to do what I do. There is nothing at home to suggest anyone who lives there is disabled. I go up stairs to bed each night without assistance. Look at my hands and the movement in my fingers!" He holds up hands that have the appearance of arthritic joints – fingers all out of line. "I can manipulate them, tie up shoe laces, wash myself, dress myself, make a cup of tea, get a little bit to eat myself. Brenda has been out at work for most of my life and I have coped. I spent three hours in the garden yesterday morning laying slabs from my chair." There were audible gasps from the congregation at this revelation.

Len leaned forward towards them as if to impart a special secret, "You can – if you want to. Where there's a will, there's a way. Whether you are fit or not, if you don't want to, you will find a good reason why you shouldn't do it, won't you? While I was working yesterday, my chair rolled down the bank with me in it and I saw stars. I thought – God! I won't be able to get to the meeting tomorrow if I'm not careful! So on the wet grass, clothes soaked, I dragged myself along the ground to sit up again. The harder blows the storm, the harder you row. You don't give in do ya?"

"I've learned patience now and I can smile. It's cost me nothing!" Len doesn't like it when the audience is quiet so he teased them again with, "It's great ain't it – aren't you all envious!" That got them laughing again – "Now where was I?" as he collected his thoughts.

"Yes, after three and a half weeks in hospital, the doctor said 'Len – you've spent enough – we are going to send you home'. I still couldn't move but I was in good shape because of my basic fitness. I was still in my plaster cast and felt a bit like the man in the iron mask. All this was to prevent me moving my neck. The day we were flown back to England, that marvellous lady, Ruth Brozy, my Angel of Berne, was waiting outside the hospital for Brenda and me. With tears in her eyes, she sprinkled us both with her very last drops of holy water from Lourdes and I remember to this day what she said. 'Mr York, the Lord will take care of you, I know. I know you will get a lot better.' Wasn't she right!"

"I replied 'I know someday that I shall be back'. At the time I was lying prostrate on the mobile bed and had no idea if I would ever get up again. But you don't let on your true feelings do you....... not when you're British. We don't start fighting until we are losing anyway, do we?"

"So three and a half weeks after setting out on a £27 holiday – we arrived back in England £863 lighter. But it's a good job I broke my neck in 1972. If I had waited until this year it would have cost me nearer £16,000. If I had waited until this year, that would have deprived me of twenty-six wonderful years. I would not swop a day with anyone because I have been so happy. If any of you could have shared the joy and happiness that I have experienced over these years, you wouldn't swop one day of your lives either!"

"We arrived at Manchester airport and I got my first two visitors – Customs and Excise Officials. They looked at my prostrate body encased in plaster, only my eyes moving, and said 'Have you anything to declare?' That brought the audience back down to earth. "Anything to declare? They couldn't even tell whether I was male or female?"

Then a young Doctor from the Robert Jones and Agnes Hunt Orthopaedic Hospital, Oswestry, introduced himself and proceeded to stab me in the bits that were uncovered, with what looked like a large safety pin. I could feel it occasionally and this prompted him to say, 'We may be able to help you a little!' This was music to my ears, 'Good Doctor,' I said, 'cos I want to go back there next year!"

"You lads" said the Doctor, "You will never learn!"

"I was twice his age and I said to him, Doctor, if you came in a car to the airport tonight, you were in a far more dangerous environment than we are in the Alps, but this was a statement on which we agreed to differ. I had eight wonderful months with him and the staff in the hospital and didn't want to leave them all when the time came."

"After three months in hospital, the neck had improved enough to allow me to sit up for one hour at a time. I had been on my back for so long that I was as stiff as an RSJ. When they sat me up I was frightened to death to turn my neck, but the nurse insisted. I turned my neck and it came back. Great – I thought I would be walking tomorrow!"

"Brenda brought me home and had to do, on her own, all the jobs that a complete staff at the hospital were employed to do. She was also working and what a brilliant job she did for me."

"After three years, she took me to Scotland – just to sit and look – not to get out. After four years I was at the 4,000 feet point on the Cairngorms. As I stood taking in the views I heard some young wag in a group of climbers saying 'What the hell is he doing up here on those crutches? Is he trying to break his neck?' Within eight years, my friends from the climbing equipment shop in Halesowen had offered to take me back to the Alps and I was proud to be standing on my own at 13,000 feet at Zermatt once more, as I had promised Ruth Brozy. I had of course, on each occasion, resorted to assistance from cable cars, – but I did it!"

"Then, in 1982, I received a letter from a lady named Alice Yates. She had attended one of my talks, and subsequently went to Zermatt. Whilst she was there she spent some time trying to find the guide who rescued me, and eventually found that she was actually staying in the hotel owned by him. Now, don't tell me it wasn't our Lord who guided her there! Ain't that a miracle? What luck again for me – I had it made didn't I? The man was an hotelier in Zermatt and when I contacted him, he made me so welcome I went to see him – and I have been to his hotel every year since. Apart from the first two visits, I have been accompanied by Brenda each year and we have had some marvellous times there. We have met most of the people who were involved including the nurse, Marie-Louise, all three guides who were on the mountain that night and the helicopter that lifted me off. We have travelled in the very same helicopter again. It is still in daily service and looks brand new. If you go to Zermatt, do have a ride in it. It is numbered HB -XDA – and you can go round the Matterhorn in it, without it costing you anything like £300 – even today."

"That's enough of my talking for now – you've passed the test. Now I will show you some pictures – that's what you've really come for I know."

He peered into the gloom of the darkened church and said "Can the lady towards the back there switch off the lights please to........." He stopped in mid-sentence as she stood up and walked to the light switch by the door. "Enable you to show your pictures more clearly?"

She had finished off the sentence for him whilst the remainder of the congregation looked on in silence. They had not known anyone was there. Len had only spotted a shadowy figure early on when she came in, but he wasn't silenced for long. It's not his nature.

"What are you doing sitting back there – why don't you come to the front with us and join the party?"

As she walked forward, Len introduced her formally, although most of the congregation had by now guessed what was happening. "Ladies and Gentlemen, we are honoured today. It is not often that my wife turns up to my meetings – she hears enough of me most days, at home – my wife Brenda." If Len had been pleased with the warmth of the reception he had been given by this small select band, he was quite overwhelmed when they stood up and clapped her, all the way to the front seats. Brenda was quite overcome by the spontaneous, rapturous applause, but managed a little curtsy and one of her most engaging smiles.

It wasn't often she caught Len napping!

As the applause died down Len said to her in a stage whisper so that all would hear. "I was aware of you when you came in but I didn't recognise you in the darkness. When you sat towards the back there I assumed you were the cleaner – I expected you to start running around with a duster any moment!"

"I will just stay for the slides," she said, "but I must leave fairly soon – you just wait until I get you home!" It was a remark that was greeted with more rapturous applause.

It took about half an hour to get through the slide show, laced with more good humour from Len. At the end, Brenda stood and said she would put on the lights on her way out, waved a farewell to them all and walked through the heavy front door of the church. She paused for a moment in the portico, to make sure she had her possessions with her. The sound from the playing of a mouth organ drifted through the doorway. It was that husband of hers again! He had become quite proficient at playing the instrument over the past couple of years and he insisted that it was "Good for the breathing." She recognised the tune.

"Alleluia, sing to Jesus
His the sceptre, his the throne"

The congregation had picked it up and were singing along with it. Even those who were not sure of the words were humming the well-known tune.

"One of our favourites" she said out loud, to herself, as she walked up the steep path to the Lychgate. She turned to look at the sandstone church in its beautiful setting. She paused to listen a moment to the third verse of the hymn.

Looking up to her left at the hill beyond she murmured, "And how we have travelled in the past hour........

Such a Long way from Clent!"